Sacred Heart
Book of Devotions

SACRED HEART
BOOK OF DEVOTIONS

Transform Your Life
with Jesus' Promises of
Graces, Peace, and Mercy

Compiled by Michael A. LaMorte
Edited by Emily Jaminet

CATHOLIC TREEHOUSE, COLUMBUS, OHIO 2022

Published by Catholic Treehouse, Columbus, Ohio
www.catholictreehouse.com

TABLE OF CONTENTS

FEAST DAY
19 DAYS AFTER PENTECOST SUNDAY

Preface

by Emily Jaminet

The one thing that is tried in true in this world is the love of Christ. Jesus came so that we can have life and have it abundantly, and this happens when our hearts welcome the love of Jesus. God offers to turn our hearts of stone to hearts of flesh, and this can only come from us encountering the Heart of Jesus.

I have discovered firsthand that this devotion is timeless and an actual spiritual stabilizer in our world, and I felt like a spiritual devotional needed to be offered to help Catholics learn to pray to Jesus and encounter His Heart through prayer.

In this devotional of ancient prayers and hymns, you will find that they will renew your faith and connect your heart with Jesus. You will see how this devotion has taken such firm root in the lives of generations before as we reveal prayers and practices that have almost been lost as it relates to the Sacred Heart. We wanted to share the very prayers that many of the laity and clergy prayed during times of war, famine, heartache, and personal trials.

What is fantastic about this prayer resource is that all of these prayers are over a hundred years or much older. When editing this devotional and reading the ancient prayers, I pictured Catholics from the 1700's and 1800's and even as far back as the early Church praying to the Heart of Jesus for a greater abundance of love. As Jesus calls us to love one another, could there be a more significant task than to do this through learning to receive the love of the Sacred Heart to heal and mend our hearts.

The timeless prayers we have assembled are an opportunity for you to reflect on the very vessel of love and mercy that flow from the Heart of Jesus. This prayer devotional is complete with papal documents, history of the devotion, consecration prayers to the Sacred Heart, First Friday Meditations, and even daily prayer and reflections for the month of June, the month dedicated to the Sacred Heart of Jesus. There are also multiple novenas and prayers that can assist you in times of struggles and strife.

Do not allow the voices of the world to define what is love; instead, choose to encounter the Heart of Jesus and allow His voice to speak to you the truth of what is love. The love from His Heart is kind, merciful, loving, and constantly inspires us to grow closer to God and be holy as God is holy.

So no matter what crosses we encounter, may we choose to embrace the Cross and discover the joy that comes from a genuine and authentic relationship with Jesus Christ through the Heart of Jesus, His Most Sacred Heart.

May you discover the peace, love, and joy that only Christ can offer.

—Emily

BY MICHAEL A. LAMORTE

The Catholic faith is one that combines the truth of Scripture and public revelation with the practice of sacred traditions passed on from generation to generation. Even the celebration of the Holy Sacrifice of the Mass contains elements that have Jewish roots. Indeed, the essence of the Catholic faith is to embrace the sacred traditions of our faith, which at their apex lies the tradition of the celebration of the Eucharist, itself rooted in the traditional Jewish celebration of the Passover feast.

As with other traditions, some sacred traditions are occasionally supplanted by new practices which become traditions themselves. As new prayers, hymns, and meditations are written and embraced, sometimes the old ones are forgotten. Not that this is necessarily a bad thing, mind you. Our faith grows like an oak tree matures from an acorn. It is ever ancient, ever new.

Yet despite new growth and new traditions, many people find great merit in practicing the traditions of Catholic Christians from ages ago. It is the strength of the faith of our ancestors—the saints who have claimed their crown—that enlivens and nourishes us in our own faith. To connect us with our forebears, these pages contain beautiful and ageless practices once forgotten so that we may join with the "great cloud of witnesses" in adoring the most precious and adorable Heart of Jesus, which was "bruised for our offenses, obedient to death, and pierced with a lance".

I pray that your devotion to the Sacred Heart of Jesus may be your "source of all consolation, your peace and reconciliation, your salvation and your hope".

—Michael

THIS HOUSE IS CONSECRATED

TO THE SACRED HEART OF JESUS

LET IT BE KNOWN THAT ON THIS _____ DAY OF _____,

IN THE YEAR OF OUR LORD _____,

THE FAMILY OF _____

CONSECRATED ITS HOUSE TO THE SACRED HEART OF JESUS

12 PROMISES OF THE SACRED HEART OF JESUS

MADE BY OUR LORD JESUS CHRIST TO SAINT MARGARET MARY ALACOQUE IN FAVOR OF PERSONS DEVOTED TO HIS DIVINE HEART

From *Little Manual of the Sacred Heart*, Joseph Schaefer, New York, 1887
+ Imprimatur: John Cardinal McCloskey, Archbishop of New York

1. "I will give them all the grace necessary for their state of life."

2. "I will establish peace in their families."

3. "I will console them in all their pains and trials."

4. "I will be their assured refuge in life and especially in death."

5. "I will shed abundant blessings upon all their undertakings."

6. "Sinners shall find in My Heart an infinite ocean of Mercy."

7. "Lukewarm souls will be rendered fervent."

8. "Fervent souls shall rise rapidly to greater perfection."

9. "I will bless every house in which an image of My Sacred Heart shall be exposed and honored."

10. "I will give to Priests the talent of moving the hardest hearts."

11. "The names of those who propagate this devotion shall be written in My Heart, from which they shall never be effaced."

12. "Publish, and cause it to be published, over all the world, that I will set no limits to My graces for those souls that come to seek them in this My Heart."

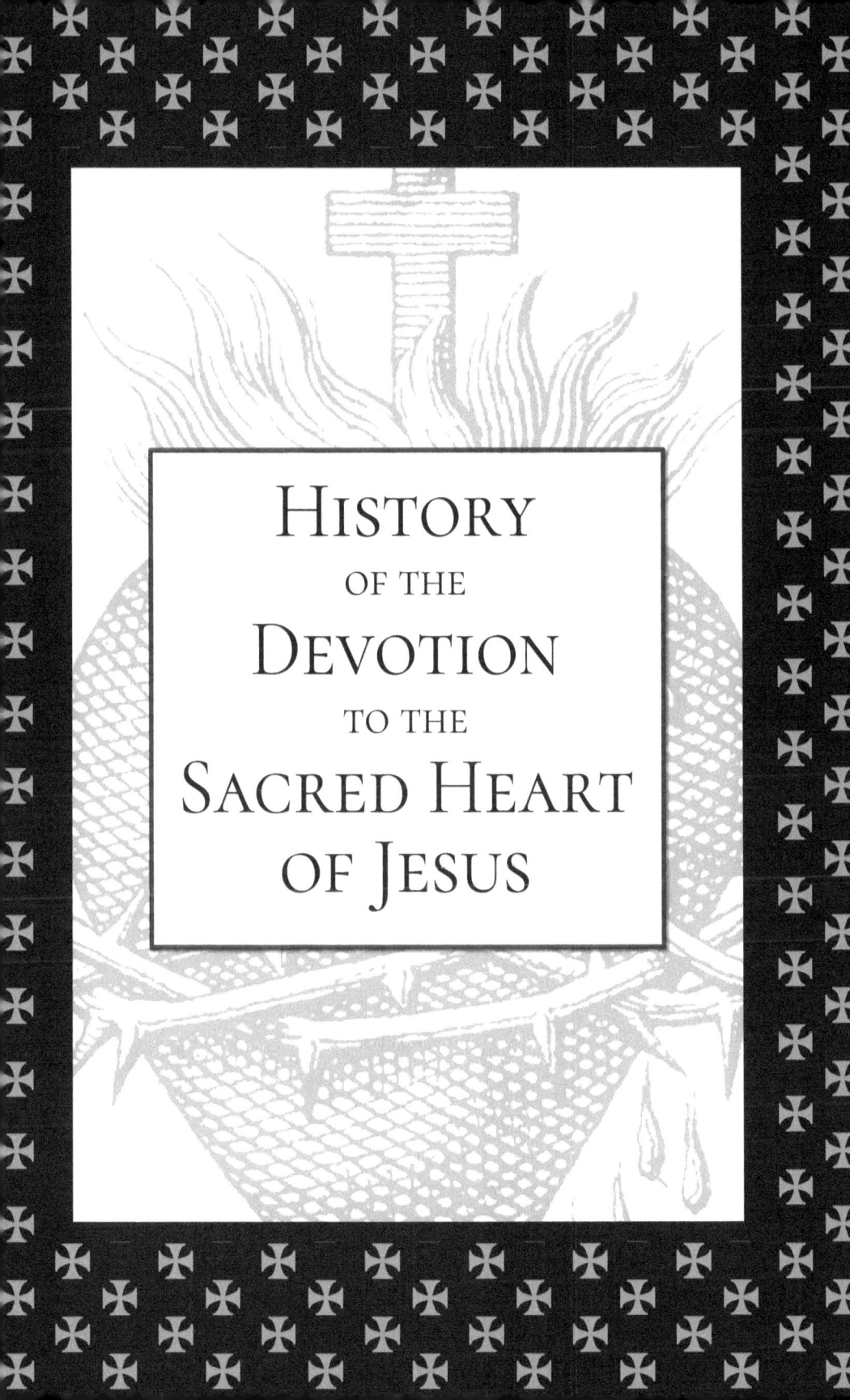

HISTORY
OF THE
DEVOTION
TO THE
SACRED HEART
OF JESUS

History of the
Devotion to the Sacred Heart of Jesus

The Origin of this Devotion

From the time of St. John and St. Paul there has always been in the Church something like devotion to the love of God, Who so loved the world as to give it his only-begotten Son, and to the love of Jesus, Who has so loved us as to deliver himself up for us. But, accurately speaking, this is not the devotion to the Sacred Heart, as it pays no homage to the Heart of Jesus as the symbol of his love for us.

From the earliest centuries, in accordance with the example of the Evangelist, Christ's open side and the mystery of blood and water were meditated upon, and the Church was beheld issuing from the side of Jesus, as Eve came forth from the side of Adam. But there is nothing to indicate that, during the first ten centuries, any worship was rendered the wounded Heart.

The Devotion Takes Root

It is in the eleventh and twelfth centuries that we find the first unmistakable indications of devotion to the Sacred Heart. Through the wound in the side the wounded Heart was gradually reached, and the wound in the Heart symbolized the wound of love.

To St. Gertrude, St. Mechtilde, and the author of the "Vitis mystica" it was already well known. Until recent times its authorship had generally been ascribed to St. Bernard and yet, by the late publishers of the beautiful and scholarly Quaracchi edition, it has been attributed, and not without plausible reasons, to St. Bonaventure ("S. Bonaventura opera omnia", 1898, VIII, LIII sq.). But, be this as it may, it contains one of the most beautiful passages that ever inspired the devotion to the Sacred Heart, one appropriated by the Church for the lessons of the second nocturn of the feast. To St. Mechtilde (d. 1298) and St. Gertrude (d. 1302) it was a familiar devotion which was translated into many beautiful prayers and exercises.

What deserves special mention is the vision of St. Gertrude on the feast of St. John the Evangelist, as it forms an epoch in the history of the devotion. Allowed to rest her head near the wound in the Savior's she heard the beating of the Divine Heart and asked

3

John if, on the night of the Last Supper, he too had felt these delightful pulsations, why he had never spoken of the fact. John replied that this revelation had been reserved for subsequent ages when the world, having grown cold, would have need of it to rekindle its love ("Legatus divinae pietatis", IV, 305; "Revelationes Gertrudianae", ed. Poitiers and Paris, 1877).

Thirteenth to Sixteen Century

From the thirteenth to the sixteenth century, the devotion was propagated but it did not seem to have developed in itself. It was everywhere practiced by privileged souls, and the lives of the saints and annals of different religious congregations, of the Franciscans, Dominicans, Carthusians, etc., furnish many examples of it. It was nevertheless a private, individual devotion of the mystical order. Nothing of a general movement had been inaugurated, unless one would so regard the propagation of the devotion to the Five Wounds, in which the Wound in the Heart figured most prominently, and for the furtherance of which the Franciscans seem to have labored.

It appears that in the sixteenth century, the devotion took an onward step and passed from the domain of mysticism into that of Christian asceticism. It was constituted an objective devotion with prayers already formulated and special exercises of which the value was extolled and the practice commended. This we learn from the writings of those two masters of the spiritual life, the pious Lanspergius (d. 1539) of the Carthusians of Cologne, and the devout Louis of Blois (Blosius; 1566), a Benedictine and Abbot of Liessies in Hainaut. To these may be added Blessed John of Avila (d. 1569) and St. Francis de Sales, the latter belonging to the seventeenth century.

From that time everything indicated an early bringing to light of the devotion. Ascetic writers spoke of it, especially those of the Society of Jesus, Alvarez de Paz, Luis de la Puente, Saint-Jure, and Nouet, and there still exist special treatises upon it such as Father Druzbicki's (d. 1662) small work, "Meta Cordium, Cor Jesu". Amongst the mystics and pious souls who practiced the devotion were St. Francis Borgia, Blessed Peter Canisius, St. Aloysius Gonzaga, and St. Alphonsus Rodriguez, of the Society of Jesus; also Venerable Marina de Escobar (d. 1633), in Spain; the Venerable Madeleine St. Joseph and the Venerable Marguerite of the Blessed Sacrament, Carmelites, in France; Jeanne de S. Mathieu Deleloe (d. 1660), a Benedictine, in Belgium; the worthy Armelle of Vannes (d. 1671); and even in Jansenistic or worldly centers, Marie de Valernod (d. 1654) and Angélique Arnauld; M. Boudon, the great archdeacon of Evreux, Father Huby, the apostle of retreats in Brittany, and, above all, the Venerable Marie de l'Incarnation, who died at Quebec in 1672. The Visitation seemed to be awaiting St. Margaret Mary; its spirituality, certain intuitions of St. Francis de Sales, the meditations of Mère l'Huillier (d. 1655), the visions of Mother Anne-Marguerite

Clément (d. 1661), and of Sister Jeanne-Bénigne Gojos (d. 1692), all paved the way. The image of the Heart of Jesus was everywhere in evidence, which fact was largely due to the Franciscan devotion to the Five Wounds and to the habit formed by the Jesuits of placing the image on their title-page of their books and the walls of their churches.

Nevertheless, the devotion remained an individual or at least a private devotion. It was reserved to St. Jean Eudes (1602-1680) to make it public, to honor it with an Office, and to establish a feast for it. Père Eudes was above all the apostle of the Heart of Mary; but in his devotion to the Immaculate Heart there was a share for the Heart of Jesus. Little by little the devotion to the Sacred Heart became a separate one, and on 31 August, 1670, the first feast of the Sacred Heart was celebrated with great solemnity in the Grand Seminary of Rennes. Coutances followed suit on 20 October, a day with which the Eudist feast was thenceforth to be connected. The feast soon spread to other dioceses, and the devotion was likewise adopted in various religious communities. Here and there it came into contact with the devotion begun at Paray, and a fusion of the two naturally resulted.

It was to Margaret Mary Alacoque (1647-1690), a humble Visitandine of the monastery at Paray-le-Monial, that Christ chose to reveal the desires of his Heart and to confide the task of imparting new life to the devotion. There is nothing to indicate that this pious religious had known the devotion prior to the revelations, or at least that she had paid any attention to it. These revelations were numerous, and the following apparitions are especially remarkable: that which occurred on the feast of St. John, when Jesus permitted Margaret Mary, as he had formerly allowed St. Gertrude, to rest her head upon his Heart, and then disclosed to her the wonders of his love, telling her that he desired to make them known to all mankind and to diffuse the treasures of his goodness, and that he had chosen her for this work (27 Dec., probably 1673); that, probably distinct from the preceding, in which he requested to be honored under the figure of his Heart of flesh; that, when he appeared radiant with love and asked for a devotion of expiatory love—frequent Communion, Communion on the First Friday of the month, and the observance of the Holy Hour (probably June or July, 1674); that known as the "great apparition" which took place during the octave of Corpus Christi, 1675, probably on 16 June, when he said, "Behold the Heart that has so loved men... instead of gratitude I receive from the greater part (of mankind) only ingratitude...", and asked her for a feast of reparation of the Friday after the octave of Corpus Christi, bidding her consult Father de la Colombière, then superior of the small Jesuit house at Paray; and finally, those in which solemn homage was asked on the part of the king, and the mission of propagating the new devotion was especially confided to the religious of the Visitation and the priests of the Society of Jesus. A few days after the "great apparition", of June, 1675, Margaret Mary made all known to Father de la

Colombière, and the latter, recognizing the action of the spirit of God, consecrated himself to the Sacred Heart, directed the holy Visitandine to write an account of the apparition, and made use of every available opportunity discreetly to circulate this account through France and England. At his death, 15 February 1682, there was found in his journal of spiritual retreats a copy in his own handwriting of the account that he had requested of Margaret Mary, together with a few reflections on the usefulness of the devotion. This journal, including the account and a beautiful "offering" to the Sacred Heart, in which the devotion was well explained, was published at Lyons in 1684. The little book was widely read, even at Paray, although not without being the cause of "dreadful confusion" to Margaret Mary, who, nevertheless, resolved to make the best of it and profited by the book for the spreading of her cherished devotion. Moulins, with Mother de Soudeilles, Dijon, with Mother de Saumaise and Sister Joly, Semur, with Mother Greyfié, and even Paray, which had at first resisted, joined the movement. Outside of the Visitandines, priests, religious, and laymen espoused the cause, particularly a Capuchin, Margaret Mary's two brothers, and some Jesuits, among the latter being Fathers Croiset and Gallifet, who were destined to do so much for the devotion.

The death of Margaret Mary, 17 October 1690, did not dampen the ardor of those interested; on the contrary, a short account of her life published by Father Croiset in 1691, as an appendix to his book "De la Dévotion au Sacré Cœur", served only to increase it. In spite of all sorts of obstacles, and of the slowness of the Holy See, which in 1693 imparted indulgences to the Confraternities of the Sacred Heart and, in 1697, granted the feast to the Visitandines with the Mass of the Five Wounds, but refused a feast common to all, with special Mass and Office, the devotion spread, particularly in religious communities. The Marseilles plague, 1720, furnished perhaps the first occasion for a solemn consecration and public worship outside of religious communities. Other cities of the South followed the example of Marseilles, and thus the devotion became a popular one. In 1726 it was deemed advisable once more to petition Rome for a feast with a Mass and Office of its own, but, in 1729, Rome again refused. However, in 1765, it finally yielded and that same year, at the request of the queen, the feast was received quasi officially by the episcopate of France. On all sides it was asked for and obtained, and finally, in 1856, at the urgent entreaties of the French bishops, Pope Pius IX extended the feast to the universal Church under the rite of double major. In 1889 it was raised by the Church to the double rite of first class. The acts of consecration and of reparation were everywhere introduced together with the devotion. Oftentimes, especially since about 1850, groups, congregations, and States have consecrated themselves to the Sacred Heart, and, in 1875, this consecration was made throughout the Catholic world. Still the pope did not wish to take the initiative or to intervene. Finally, on 11 June, 1899, by order of Leo XIII, and with the formula prescribed by him, all mankind was solemnly consecrated to the Sacred Heart. The idea of this act, which Leo XIII called "the great act" of his pontificate, had been proposed to him by a religious of the Good Shepherd from Oporto (Portugal) who said that she had received it from Christ himself. She was a member of the Drost-zu-Vischering family, and known in religion as Sister Mary of the Divine Heart. She died on the feast of the Sacred Heart, two days before the consecration, which had been deferred to the following Sunday. Whilst alluding to these great public manifestations we must not omit referring to the intimate life of the devotion in souls, to the practices connected with it, and to the works and associations of which it was the very life. Moreover, we must not overlook the social character which it has assumed particularly of late years. The Catholics of France, especially, cling firmly to it as one of their strongest hopes of ennoblement and salvation.

EXCERPTED & ADAPTED FROM: Bainvel, J. (1910). Devotion to the Sacred Heart of Jesus. In *The Catholic Encyclopedia*. New York: Robert Appleton Company. Retrieved April 26, 2021 from New Advent: *http://www.newadvent.org/cathen/07163a.htm*

FIRST IMAGE OF THE SACRED HEART BY ST. MARGARET MARY

Copie authentique de la PREMIÈRE IMAGE DU SACRÉ CŒUR VENÉRÉE par SAINTE MARGUERITE. MARIE, en 1685, au Monastère de Paray-le-Monial.

"I saw this divine Heart as on a throne of flames, more brilliant than the sun and transparent as crystal. It has its adorable wound and was encircled with a crown of thorns, which signified the pricks our sins caused him. It was surmounted by a cross."

The Pastoral Letter
of the Bishop of Boulogne, France

17 July 1765

Our august Queen [Mary Lecksinska, Princess of Poland, Queen of France], my dear brethren! with making that pious devotion to which we invite you, (to which she herself glories to be associated, and which reigns with her on the throne) takes a pride and pleasure in spreading it over the face of the whole kingdom of France. As she has leant in the school of Christ the admirable invention of reconciling the humility of the heart with the elevation of the soul, it is not enough for this incomparable princess to resemble the pious Esther, who, preserving the love of holy abjection, even at the highest pitch of her glory, deplored her being constrained to appear in public with a diadem on her head, and delighted to lay down in private her scepter and crown at the feet of her Creator; she is also willing to walk in the footsteps of St. Clotilda, who, procuring the conversion of the first of our most Christian kings, conceived at the same time the noble design of subjugating the whole French nation to the yoke of Jesus Christ. The design of our august queen is yet more sublime, since she intends nothing less than to enlarge the empire of divine love, and to make it flourish in all her dominions, by establishing a devotion, whose chief end is to bring all her people under the subjection of the sacred heart of her Lord and God, and to inflame their hearts as well as her own with the fire of his love.

It was to our age and nation the divine providence was pleased to reserve the honor and glory, to seal, as it were, all those solemnities by the general and perpetual establishment of the pious devotion to the Sacred Heart of our Lord Jesus Christ, which is already spread through the several dioceses in France, in the capital city of the Christian world, in all the Catholic countries, and even in China, and in the East and West Indies. It has had the sanction of the most learned doctors, and has been approved of by many illustrious persons and chief bishops, who have granted indulgences to its followers, amongst whom we may reckon many persons of the most eminent virtue, great personages of the world, several princesses of the blood, and many crowned heads.

When in 1720 one of the most flourishing provinces of France was desolated by pestilence [the bubonic plague], and many of its inhabitants fell a daily prey to this malignant contagion, as soon as the bishops of Provence, the magistrates and citizens

QUEEN MARY LECZINSKA PAYS HOMAGE TO THE SACRED HEART OF JESUS & THE EUCHARIST

of Marseilles, Arles, Aix and Toulon dedicated themselves by a solemn oath to the worship of the sacred heart of Jesus, these cities were immediately delivered from the dreadful plague and with which they were afflicted. Such is the esteem we have entertained of this devotion, that upon mature deliberation we wish heartily to establish and spread it throughout our whole diocese.

Would to God, my dear brethren! that to induce you more effectually to the embracing such an advantageous devotion, we were endowed with greater abilities to treat in a worthy manner so sublime a subject, for which the most pathetic and moving eloquence is required: that we were animated with the tender piety of St. Bernard, and supplied with the insinuating unction, and the persuasive charms of his eloquence: but were we enriched with all those endowments, were we speaking with the tongues of prophets, of the apostles, and even of angels, we could neither attain all the prerogatives, nor worthily express all the allurements and precious advantages of this devotion. In what ever light it may be considered, what do we perceive in it but a tendency to display the wonderful bounty is of God for men, that should triumph over the hardness of their insensible hearts by the love of his own, to deliver them from the tyranny of their imperious passions, and the slavery of the most shameful vices, in order to bring them under the glorious and happy dominion of the queen of all virtues.

What is the corporal and sensible object of this devotion? It is the material heart of the Son of God who was made man out of his pure love for us; it is the most noble part of his adorable body; it is the principal organ of all the affections, and consequently of all the virtues of his blessed humanity; it is the seat and center where corporally dwells all the plenitude of his dignity and which becoming by virtue of the hypostatical union the heart of the King of kings, of the Holy of holies, of the God majesty, is raised to an infinite dignity which makes it worthy of our profound homage and adoration. Ah! If the lance with which the side of Jesus was opened upon the cross is by that very touch becomes subject of veneration to all the Catholic world, how much more venerable ought to be his sacred heart, which conferred so much dignity on this low, mean, and contemptible piece of steel. If the precious ointment poured by Magdalen on the feet of our Redeemer was so acceptable to him as to deserve his commendation and a magnificent reward, how much more highly will he approve of a plentifully recompense the honor which is paid to his heart, whose motions were always so perfectly conformable to the sentiments either of the love or zeal which burnt in his sacred breast, or of the sadness and anguish with which his soul was overwhelmed and more contributed than those of another part of his body to the most wonderful production of his divine mercy, the great work of our redemption.

Excerpted from *The Devotion & Office of the Sacred Heart of our Lord Jesus Christ*, 12th Edition, Keating & Brown, London, 1821

ANNUM SACRUM

ENCYCLICAL OF POPE LEO XIII ON CONSECRATION TO THE SACRED HEART

25 May 1899

To the Patriarchs, Primates, Archbishops, and Bishops of the Catholic World in Grace and Communion with the Apostolic See.

Venerable Brethren, Health and Apostolic Benediction.

But a short time ago, as you well know, We, by letters apostolic, and following the custom and ordinances of Our predecessors, commanded the celebration in this city, at no distant date, of a Holy Year. And now today, in the hope and with the object that this religious celebration shall be more devoutly performed, We have traced and recommended a striking design from which, if all shall follow it out with hearty good will, We not unreasonably expect extraordinary and lasting benefits for Christendom in the first place and also for the whole human race.

2. Already more than once We have endeavored, after the example of Our predecessors Innocent XII, Benedict XIII, Clement XIII, Pius VI, and Pius IX., devoutly to foster and bring out into fuller light that most excellent form of devotion which has for its object the veneration of the Sacred Heart of Jesus; this We did especially by the Decree given on June 28, 1889, by which We raised the Feast under that name to the dignity of the first class. But now We have in mind a more signal form of devotion which shall be in a manner the crowning perfection of all the honors that people have been accustomed to pay to the Sacred Heart, and which We confidently trust will be most pleasing to Jesus Christ, our Redeemer. This is not the first time,

however, that the design of which We speak has been mooted. Twenty-five years ago, on the approach of the solemnities of the second centenary of the Blessed Margaret Mary Alacoque's reception of the Divine command to propagate the worship of the Sacred Heart, many letters from all parts, not merely from private persons but from Bishops also were sent to Pius IX. begging that he would consent to consecrate the whole human race to the Most Sacred Heart of Jesus. It was thought best at the time to postpone the matter in order that a well-considered decision might be arrived at. Meanwhile permission was granted to individual cities which desired it thus to consecrate themselves, and a form of consecration was drawn up. Now, for certain new and additional reasons, We consider that the plan is ripe for fulfillment.

3. This world-wide and solemn testimony of allegiance and piety is especially appropriate to Jesus Christ, who is the Head and Supreme Lord of the race. his empire extends not only over Catholic nations and those who, having been duly washed in the waters of holy baptism, belong of right to the Church, although erroneous opinions keep them astray, or dissent from her teaching cuts them off from her care; it comprises also all those who are deprived of the Christian faith, so that the whole human race is most truly under the power of Jesus Christ. For he who is the Only-begotten Son of God the Father, having the same substance with him and being the brightness of his glory and the figure of his substance (Hebrews 1:3) necessarily has everything in common with the Father, and therefore sovereign power over all things. This is why the Son of God thus speaks of himself through the Prophet: "But I am appointed king by him over Sion, his holy mountain... The Lord said to me, Thou art my son, this day have I begotten thee. Ask of me and I will give thee the Gentiles for thy inheritance and the utmost parts of the earth for thy possession" (Psalm 2). By these words he declares that he has power from God over the whole Church, which is signified by Mount Sion, and also over the rest of the world to its uttermost ends. On what foundation this sovereign power rests is made sufficiently plain by the words, "Thou art My Son." For by the very fact that he is the Son of the King of all, he is also the heir of all his Father's power: hence the words—"I will give thee the Gentiles for thy inheritance," which are similar to those used by Paul the Apostle, "whom he bath appointed heir of all things" (Hebrews 1:2).

4. But we should now give most special consideration to the declarations made by Jesus Christ, not through the Apostles or the Prophets but by his own words. To the Roman Governor who asked him, "Art thou a king then?" he answered unhesitatingly, "Thou sayest that I am a king" (John 18:37). And

the greatness of this power and the boundlessness of his kingdom is still more clearly declared in these words to the Apostles: "All power is given to me in heaven and on earth" (Matthew 28:18). If then all power has been given to Christ it follows of necessity that his empire must be supreme, absolute and independent of the will of any other, so that none is either equal or like unto it: and since it has been given in heaven and on earth it ought to have heaven and earth obedient to it. And verily he has acted on this extraordinary and peculiar right when he commanded his Apostles to preach his doctrine over the earth, to gather all men together into the one body of the Church by the baptism of salvation, and to bind them by laws, which no one could reject without risking his eternal salvation.

5. But this is not all. Christ reigns nor only by natural right as the Son of God, but also by a right that he has acquired. For he it was who snatched us "from the power of darkness" (Colossians 1:13), and "gave himself for the redemption of all" (I Timothy 2:6). Therefore not only Catholics, and those who have duly received Christian baptism, but also all men, individually and collectively, have become to him "a purchased people" (I Peter 2:9). St. Augustine's words are therefore to the point when he says: "You ask what price he paid? See what he gave and you will understand how much he paid. The price was the blood of Christ. What could cost so much but the whole world, and all its people? The great price he paid was paid for all" (T. 120 on St. John).

6. How it comes about that infidels themselves are subject to the power and dominion of Jesus Christ is clearly shown by St. Thomas, who gives us the reason and its explanation. For having put the question whether his judicial power extends to all men, and having stated that judicial authority flows naturally from royal authority, he concludes decisively as follows: "All things are subject to Christ as far as his power is concerned, although they are not all subject to him in the exercise of that power" (3a., p., q. 59, a. 4). This sovereign power of Christ over men is exercised by truth, justice, and above all, by charity.

7. To this twofold ground of his power and domination he graciously allows us, if we think fit, to add voluntary consecration. Jesus Christ, our God and our Redeemer, is rich in the fullest and perfect possession of all things: we, on the other hand, are so poor and needy that we have nothing of our own to offer him as a gift. But yet, in his infinite goodness and love, he in no way objects to our giving and consecrating to him what is already His, as if it were really our own; nay, far from refusing such an offering, he positively

desires it and asks for it: "My son, give me thy heart." We are, therefore, able to be pleasing to him by the good will and the affection of our soul. For by consecrating ourselves to him we not only declare our open and free acknowledgment and acceptance of his authority over us, but we also testify that if what we offer as a gift were really our own, we would still offer it with our whole heart. We also beg of him that he would vouchsafe to receive it from us, though clearly his own. Such is the efficacy of the act of which We speak, such is the meaning underlying Our words.

8. And since there is in the Sacred Heart a symbol and a sensible image of the infinite love of Jesus Christ which moves us to love one another, therefore is it fit and proper that we should consecrate ourselves to his most Sacred Heart-an act which is nothing else than an offering and a binding of oneself to Jesus Christ, seeing that whatever honor, veneration and love is given to this divine Heart is really and truly given to Christ himself.

9. For these reasons We urge and exhort all who know and love this divine Heart willingly to undertake this act of piety; and it is Our earnest desire that all should make it on the same day, that so the aspirations of so many thousands who are performing this act of consecration may be borne to the temple of heaven on the same day. But shall We allow to slip from Our remembrance those innumerable others upon whom the light of Christian truth has not yet shined? We hold the place of him who came to save that which was lost, and who shed his blood for the salvation of the whole human race. And so We greatly desire to bring to the true life those who sit in the shadow of death. As we have already sent messengers of Christ over the earth to instruct them, so now, in pity for their lot with all Our soul we commend them, and as far as in us lies We consecrate them to the Sacred Heart of Jesus. In this way this act of devotion, which We recommend, will be a blessing to all. For having performed it, those in whose hearts are the knowledge and love of Jesus Christ will feel that faith and love increased. Those who knowing Christ, yet neglect his law and its precepts, may still gain from his Sacred Heart the flame of charity. And lastly, for those still more unfortunate, who are struggling in the darkness of superstition, we shall all with one mind implore the assistance of heaven that Jesus Christ, to whose power they are subject, may also one day render them submissive to its exercise; and that not only in the life to come when he will fulfill his will upon all men, by saving some and punishing others, (St. Thomas, ibid), but also in this mortal life by giving them faith and holiness. May they by these virtues strive to honor God as they ought, and to win everlasting happiness in heaven.

10. Such an act of consecration, since it can establish or draw tighter the bonds which naturally connect public affairs with God, gives to States a hope of better things. In these latter times especially, a policy has been followed which has resulted in a sort of wall being raised between the Church and civil society. In the constitution and administration of States the authority of sacred and divine law is utterly disregarded, with a view to the exclusion of religion from having any constant part in public life. This policy almost tends to the removal of the Christian faith from our midst, and, if that were possible, of the banishment of God himself from the earth. When men's minds are raised to such a height of insolent pride, what wonder is it that the greater part of the human race should have fallen into such disquiet of mind and be buffeted by waves so rough that no one is suffered to be free from anxiety and peril? When religion is once discarded it follows of necessity that the surest foundations of the public welfare must give way, whilst God, to inflict on his enemies the punishment they so richly deserve, has left them the prey of their own evil desires, so that they give themselves up to their passions and finally wear themselves out by excess of liberty.

11. Hence that abundance of evils which have now for a long time settled upon the world, and which pressingly call upon us to seek for help from him by whose strength alone they can be driven away. Who can he be but Jesus Christ the Only-begotten Son of God? "For there is no other name under heaven given to men whereby we must be saved" (Acts 4:12). We must have recourse to him who is the Way, the Truth and the Life. We have gone astray and we must return to the right path: darkness has overshadowed our minds, and the gloom must be dispelled by the light of truth: death has seized upon us, and we must lay hold of life. It will at length be possible that our many wounds be healed and all justice spring forth again with the hope of restored authority; that the splendors of peace be renewed, and swords and arms drop from the hand when all men shall acknowledge the empire of Christ and willingly obey his word, and "Every tongue shall confess that our Lord Jesus Christ is in the glory of God the Father" (Philippians 2:11).

12. When the Church, in the days immediately succeeding her institution, was oppressed beneath the yoke of the Caesars, a young Emperor saw in the heavens across, which became at once the happy omen and cause of the glorious victory that soon followed. And now, today, behold another blessed and heavenly token is offered to our sight—the most Sacred Heart of Jesus, with a cross rising from it and shining forth with dazzling splendor amidst

flames of love. In that Sacred Heart all our hopes should be placed, and from it the salvation of men is to be confidently besought.

13. Finally, there is one motive which We are unwilling to pass over in silence, personal to Ourselves it is true, but still good and weighty, which moves Us to undertake this celebration. God, the author of every good, not long ago preserved Our life by curing Us of a dangerous disease. We now wish, by this increase of the honor paid to the Sacred Heart, that the memory of this great mercy should be brought prominently forward, and Our gratitude be publicly acknowledged.

14. For these reasons, We ordain that on the ninth, tenth and eleventh of the coming month of June, in the principal church of every town and village, certain prayers be said, and on each of these days there be added to the other prayers the Litany of the Sacred Heart approved by Our authority. On the last day the form of consecration shall be recited which, Venerable Brethren, We sent to you with these letters.

15. As a pledge of divine benefits, and in token of Our paternal benevolence, to you, and to the clergy and people committed to your care We lovingly grant in the Lord the Apostolic Benediction.

Given in Rome at St. Peter's on the 25th day of May, 1899, the twenty-second year of Our Pontificate.

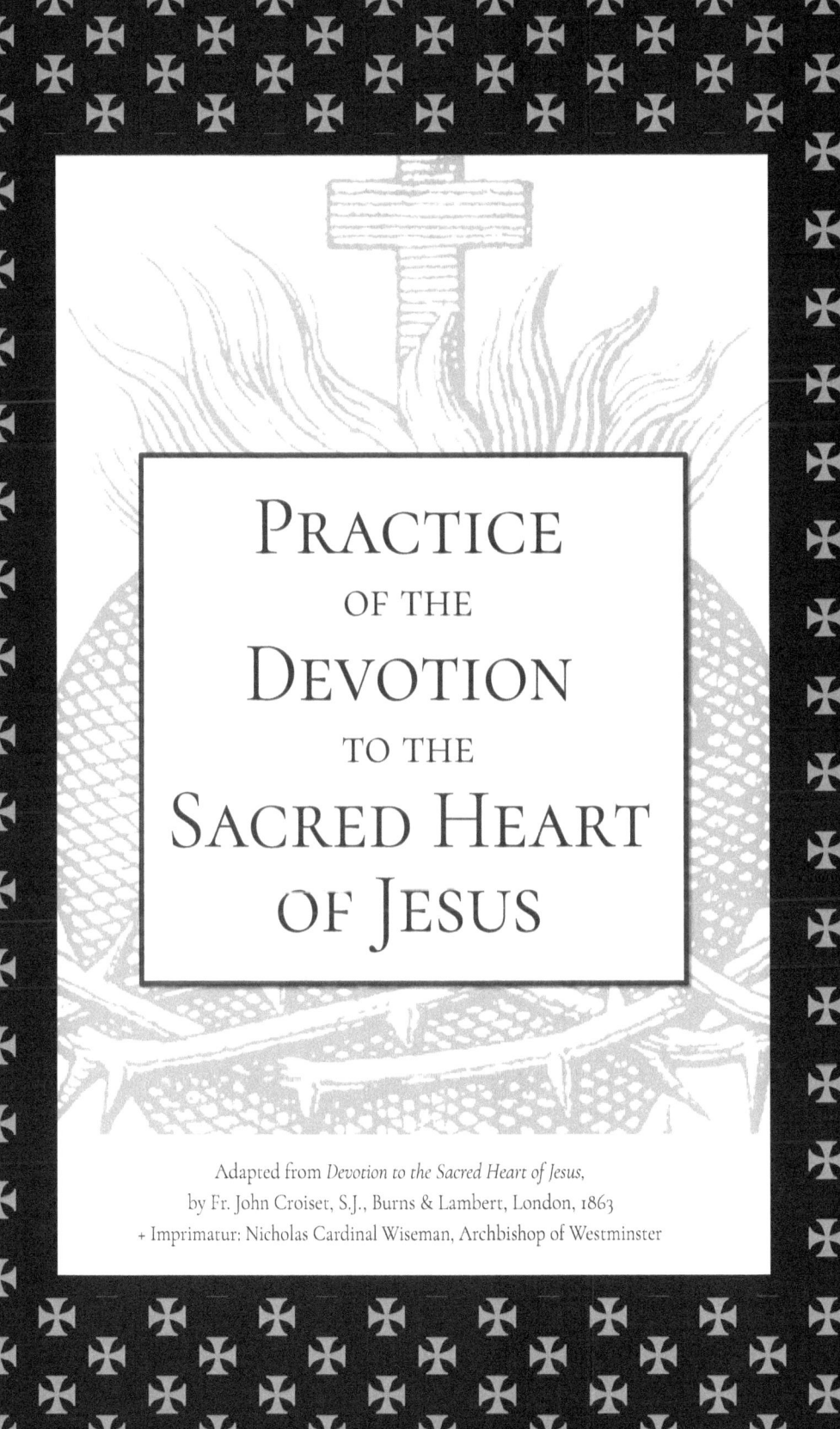

PRACTICE

OF THE

DEVOTION

TO THE

SACRED HEART

OF JESUS

Adapted from *Devotion to the Sacred Heart of Jesus,*
by Fr. John Croiset, S.J., Burns & Lambert, London, 1863
+ Imprimatur: Nicholas Cardinal Wiseman, Archbishop of Westminster

The Feast

Every year, the solemn festival of his devotion is fixed on the first Friday after the octave of Corpus Christi. This day must be sanctified and consecrated to the love of our blessed Savior by prayer, pious reading, visits to the blessed sacrament, and every good work and therefore, on the eve of this solemn day, prepare your heart, by some act of penance or charity, for the reception of divine grace.

On the festival itself, make acts of reparation by way of the sacraments of Penance and Holy Communion. At confession, accuse yourself and detest in a special manner your many ingratitudes and acts of disrespect towards the blessed sacrament. Your communion ought to be performed with so much the more fervor, as it is intended as a reparation of honor, and an atonement for the many negligences and defects in former communions.

During the day, if convenient, pay a special visit to the blessed sacrament, and there, or in your oratory, at the foot of the crucifix, make a solemn act of atonement to the sacred heart for all the indignities it daily receives in the blessed Eucharist, and for such as we ourselves perhaps have been guilty of.

Every Day And In The Morning

Every morning, as soon as you awake, throw yourself in spirit into that divine heart which so mercifully watched over you whilst you were asleep. Thank Jesus Christ for the institution of the most blessed sacrament; adore that most amiable Savior, love him most tenderly, and entreat your angel guardian to visit him for you. When dressed, turning your mind towards the chapel where the blessed sacrament is kept, make a profound reverence, resolved to present yourself there in person with all proper convenience. In the meanwhile, make the following act of adoration:

Jesus Christ, my Lord and my God! Whom I believe is truly and really present in the blessed sacrament of the altar, receive this my homage, and let it supply for the desire I have of adoring thee without intermission, and in return for those sentiments of love which thy sacred heart express for us in the ever-adorable sacrament.

Every Week

The zealous clients of this devotion, who endeavor to procure for themselves a more plentiful flow of heavenly graces, are not satisfied with honoring this divine heart once a month; they more over consecrate the Friday of every week to its honor, by the performance of some acts of devotion, some good works, or small mortifications, interior or exterior, it in order to testify their gratitude, and repair by their love the ingratitude of men to Jesus Christ.

Every Month

Besides the principal festival, which happens but once a year, the first Friday of every month has been also consecrated to the sacred heart. On that day the clients endeavor to perform, either wholly or in part, the religious duties practiced on the feast itself, such as confession, communion, visits to the blessed sacrament, and the reparation of honor.

The Sacred Heart on a Cloth Held by an Angel, circa 1480–90

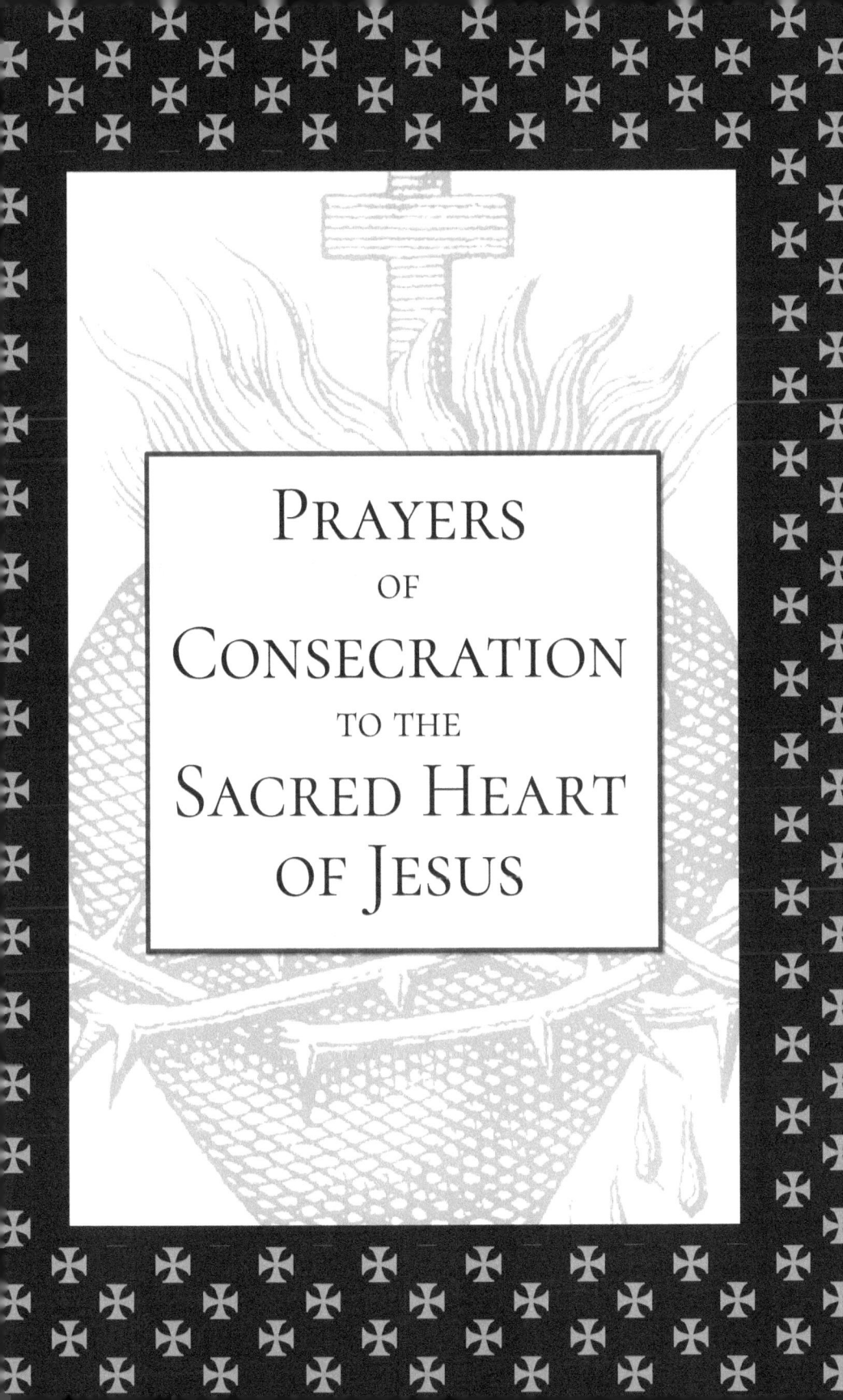

PRAYERS

OF

CONSECRATION

TO THE

SACRED HEART

OF JESUS

ACT OF CONSECRATION OF THE HUMAN RACE TO THE SACRED HEART OF JESUS

BY POPE PIUS XI

Most sweet Jesus, Redeemer of the human race, look down upon us, humbly prostrate before Thine altar. We are Thine and Thine we wish to be; but to be more surely united with Thee, behold each one of us freely consecrates himself today to Thy Most Sacred Heart. Many, indeed, have never known Thee; many, too, despising Thy precepts, have rejected Thee. Have mercy on them all, most merciful Jesus, and draw them to Thy Sacred Heart.

Be Thou King, O Lord, not only of the faithful who have never forsaken Thee, but also of the prodigal children who have abandoned Thee, grant that they may quickly return to their Father's house, lest they die of wretchedness and hunger.

Be Thou King of those who are deceived by erroneous opinions, or whom discord keeps aloof and call them back to the harbor of truth and unity of faith, so that soon there may be but one flock and one shepherd.

Be Thou King of all those who even now sit in the shadow of idolatry or Islam, and refuse not Thou to bring them into the light of Thy kingdom. Look, finally, with eyes of pity upon the children of that race, which was for so long a time Thy chosen people; and let Thy Blood, which was once invoked upon them in vengeance, now descend upon them also in a cleansing flood of redemption and eternal life.

Grant, O Lord, to Thy Church, assurance of freedom and immunity from harm; give peace and order to all nations, and make the earth resound from pole to pole with one cry: Praise to the Divine Heart that wrought our salvation: to it be glory and honor forever. Amen.

A Solemn Act of Consecration to The Sacred Heart of Jesus

by Saint Margaret Mary Alacoque

I give myself and consecrate to the Sacred Heart of our Lord Jesus Christ, my person and my life, my actions, pains and sufferings, so that I may be unwilling to make use of any part of my being other than to honor, love and glorify the Sacred Heart.

This is my unchanging purpose, namely, to be all His, and to do all things for the love of him, at the same time renouncing with all my heart whatever is displeasing to him.

I therefore take you, O Sacred Heart, to be the only object of my love, the guardian of my life, my assurance of salvation, the remedy of my weakness and inconstancy, the atonement for all the faults of my life and my sure refuge at the hour of death.

Be then, O Heart of goodness, my justification before God the Father, and turn away from me the strokes of his righteous anger.

O Heart of love, I put all my confidence in you, for I fear everything from my own wickedness and frailty, but I hope for all things from your goodness and bounty.

Remove from me all that can displease you or resist your holy will; let your pure love imprint your image so deeply upon my heart, that I shall never be able to forget you or to be separated from you.

May I obtain from all your loving kindness the grace of having my name written in your Heart, for in you I desire to place all my happiness and glory, living and dying in bondage to you. Amen.

DAILY RENEWAL OF THE CONSECRATION TO THE SACRED HEART OF JESUS

Dear Sacred Heart of Jesus,
we renew our pledge of love and loyalty to you.

Keep us always close to your loving Heart
and to the most pure heart of your mother.

May we love one another more and more each day,
forgiving each other's faults as you forgive our sins.

Teach us how to see you in those we meet outside our home.

Please help us keep our love for you always strong
by frequent Mass and Communion.

Thank you, dear Jesus, King and Friend of our family,
for all the blessings of today.

Protect us during this night.

Help us all to get to Heaven! Amen.

Most Sacred Heart of Jesus, Thy Kingdom come!

Immaculate Heart of Mary, pray for our family!

St. Joseph, friend of the Sacred Heart, pray for us!

Our patron saints and guardian angels, pray for us!

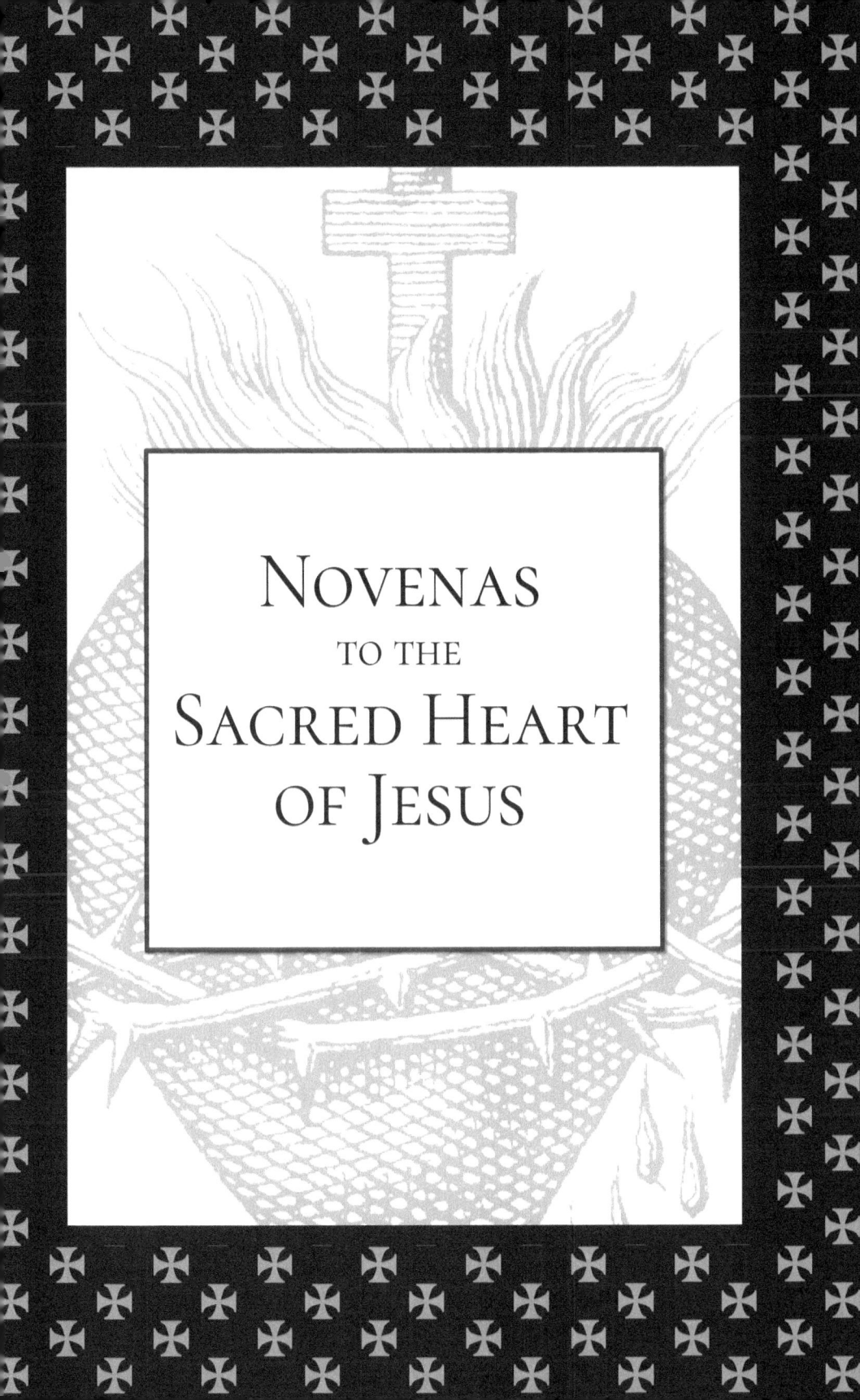

NOVENAS

TO THE

SACRED HEART

OF JESUS

Rules for the Proper Observance of Novenas
By St. Alphonses de Liguori

1. The soul must be in the state of grace; for the devotion of a sinful heart pleases neither God nor the saints.

2. We must persevere, that is, the prayers for each day of the novena must never be omitted.

3. If possible, we should visit a church every day, and there implore the favor we desire.

4. Every day we ought to perform certain specified acts of exterior self-denial and interior mortification, in order to prepare us thereby for the reception of grace.

5. It is most important that we receive holy communion when making a novena. Therefore prepare yourself well for it.

6. After obtaining the desired grace for which the novena was made, do not omit to return thanks to God and to the saint through whose intercession your prayers were heard.

A Short Novena to the Sacred Heart of Jesus
Say the following prayer 6 times per day for 9 consecutive days.

May the Sacred Heart of Jesus be loved and adored in all the tabernacles of the world now and forever. May the Sacred Heart of Jesus be loved and glorified until the end of all time. Saint Jude... *pray for us and hear our prayers.*

Holy Heart Prayer Novena

O most holy Heart of Jesus, fountain of every blessing, I adore you, I love you and with a lively sorrow for my sins, I offer you this poor heart of mine. Make me humble, patient, pure and wholly obedient to your will. Grant, good Jesus, that I may live in you and for you. Protect me in the midst of danger; comfort me in my afflictions; give me health of body, assistance in my temporal needs, your blessing on all that I do, and the grace of a holy death. Within your Heart I place my every care. In every need let me come to you with humble trust saying, "Heart of Jesus help me." Merciful Jesus, I consecrate myself today and always to your most Sacred Heart. Most Sacred Heart of Jesus I implore, that I may ever love you more and more. Most Sacred Heart of Jesus, *I trust in you.* Most Sacred Heart of Jesus, *have mercy on us!* Sacred Heart of Jesus, *I believe in your love for me.* Jesus, meek and humble of heart, *make my heart like unto Thine.* Sacred Heart of Jesus, *Thy Kingdom Come.* Most Sacred Heart of Jesus, *convert sinners, save the dying, deliver the Holy Souls in Purgatory.* Amen.

Novena to the Sacred Heart Version I

Divine Jesus, you have said, "Ask and you shall receive; seek and you shall find; knock and it shall be opened to you." Behold me kneeling at your feet, filled with a lively faith and confidence in the promises dictated by your Sacred Heart to Saint Margaret Mary.

I come to ask this favor: *(State your intention)*

To whom can I turn if not to you, whose Heart is the source of all graces and merits? Where should I seek if not in the treasure which contains all the riches of your kindness and mercy? Where should I knock if not at the door through which God gives himself to us and through which we go to God? I have recourse to you, Heart of Jesus. In you I find consolation when afflicted, protection when persecuted, strength when burdened with trials, and light in doubt and darkness.

Dear Jesus, I firmly believe that you can grant me the grace I implore, even though it should require a miracle. You have only to will it and my prayer will be granted. I admit that I am most unworthy of your favors, but this is not a reason for me to be discouraged. You are the God of mercy, and you will not refuse a contrite heart. Cast upon me a look of mercy, I beg of you, and your kind Heart will find in my miseries and weakness a reason for granting my prayer.

Sacred Heart, whatever may be your decision with regard to my request, I will never stop adoring, loving, praising, and serving you. My Jesus, be pleased to accept this my act of perfect resignation to the decrees of your adorable Heart, which I sincerely desire may be fulfilled in and by me and all your creatures forever. Grant me the grace for which I humbly implore you through the Immaculate Heart of your most sorrowful Mother. You entrusted me to her as her child, and her prayers are all-powerful with you.

Amen

Novena to the Sacred Heart Version II

O Sacred and adorable Heart of Jesus! Furnace of Eternal charity! Ocean of infinite mercy! Consolation of the afflicted! Refuge of sinners and hope of the whole world! I most fervently adore you, and unite my heart, my affections, and supplications, to the perpetual homage that you render to the divinity on our altars.

Most amiable Heart, which has loved us with an eternal love, supply yourself for my insensibility, and receive my desire at least of loving you with all the ardor and sincerity you so justly merit. But remember, O adorable Heart! that you have not disclosed yourself to us only as an object of our adorations; you desire much more to engage our love, and to become the ground and motive of our loving confidence. For this end, you were pierced through with a lance on the Cross; and for the same purpose you remain a daily victim of your own love on our altars.

O infinitely compassionate Heart of Jesus which was overwhelmed with sorrow in the Garden of Olives, at the view of our spiritual and corporal miseries, I recur of you now with all the confidence you desire I should have in the extent of your power and the riches of your mercy. Convinced that those things which are impossible to human beings are infinitely easy to you, and relying with a humble steadfast faith on the sacred words of truth itself, that whatever we ask the Father in the Name of Jesus should be granted, I now most humbly implore in that adorable Name, in virtue of that promise, and through the abundant mercies of the Sacred Heart of Jesus, the particular favor I petition for in this Novena: *(State your intention).*

O blessed Saint Gertrude and all you glorious servants of Christ; who while on earth were particularly devoted to the Sacred Heart of Jesus, join your prayers with mine, and implore from the Divine Object of all your devotion the obtaining of the petition which I now make, and specially offer up through your intercession. Beg likewise, from this adorable Heart, which has dominion over all hearts, and could in a moment change the most stubborn, to have compassion on those who are in the dreadful state of mortal sin, and to open to us the treasure of its mercy at the hour of our death.

Amen

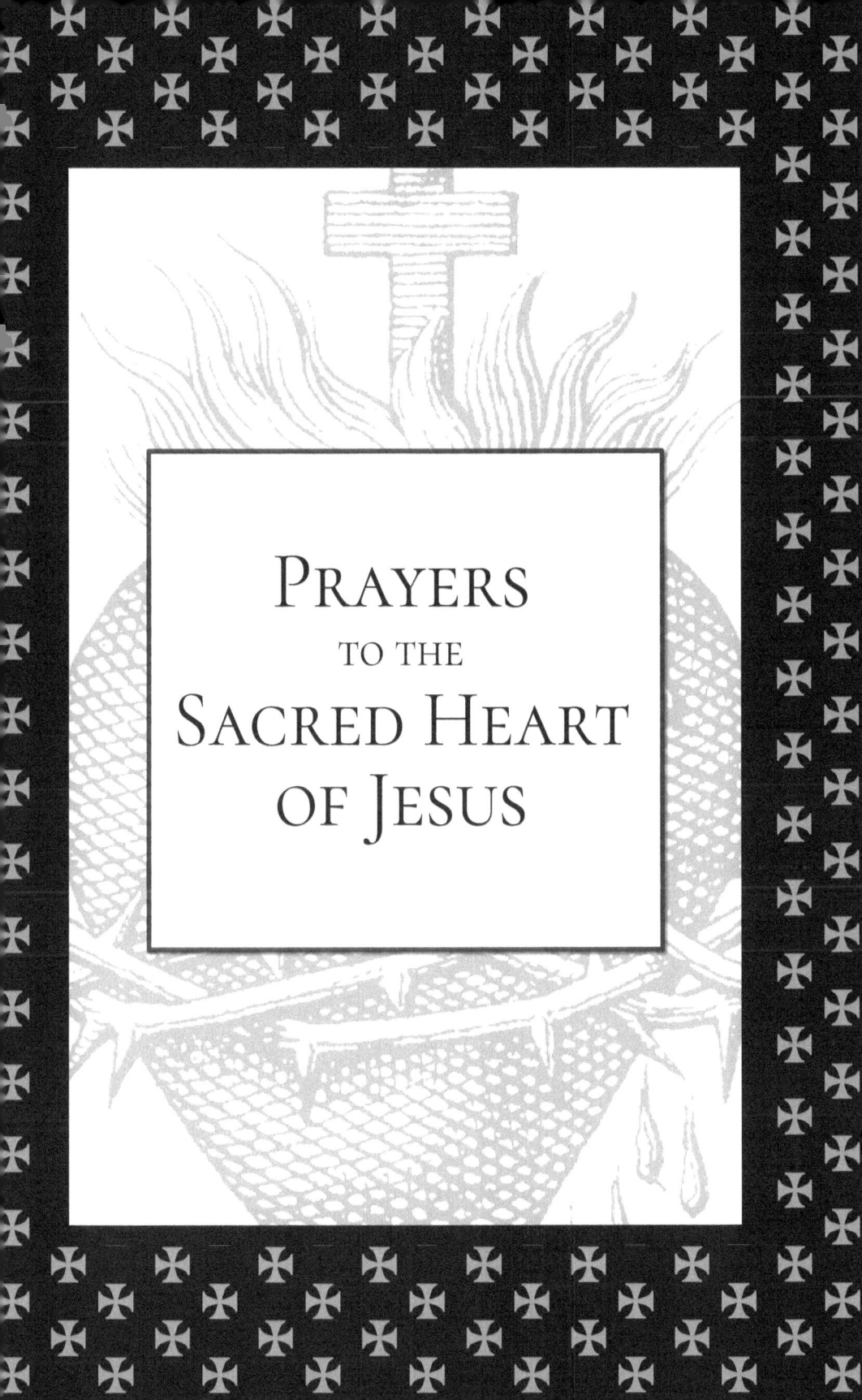

Prayers
to the
Sacred Heart
of Jesus

A Salutation to the Sacred Heart

by Saint Margaret Mary Alacoque

Hail, Heart of Jesus, *save me!*

Hail, Heart of my Creator, *perfect me!*

Hail, Heart of my Savior, *deliver me!*

Hail, Heart of my Judge, *grant me pardon!*

Hail, Heart of my Father, *govern me!*

Hail, Heart of my Spouse, *grant me love!*

Hail, Heart of my Master, *teach me!*

Hail, Heart of my King, *be my crown!*

Hail, Heart of my Benefactor, *enrich me!*

Hail, Heart of my Shepherd, *guard me!*

Hail, Heart of my Friend, *comfort me!*

Hail, Heart of my Brother, *stay with me!*

Hail, Heart of the Child Jesus, *draw me to Thyself!*

Hail, Heart of Jesus dying on the Cross, *redeem me!*

Hail, Heart of Jesus in all Thy states, *give Thyself to me!*

Hail, Heart of incomparable goodness, *have mercy on me!*

Hail, Heart of splendor, *shine within me!*

Hail, most loving Heart, *inflame me!*

Hail, most merciful Heart, *work within me!*

Hail, most humble Heart, *dwell within me!*

Hail, most patient Heart, *support me!*

Hail, most faithful Heart, *be my reward!*

Hail, most admirable and most worthy Heart, *bless me!*

LITANY OF THE SACRED HEART OF JESUS

COMPOSED BY POPE LEO XIII

V: Lord, have mercy on us.

R: *Christ, have mercy on us.*

Lord, have mercy on us. Christ, hear us.
Christ, graciously hear us.

God the Father of Heaven, †*have mercy on us.*

God the Son, Redeemer of the world†

God, the Holy Spirit†

Holy Trinity, One God†

Heart of Jesus, Son of the Eternal Father†

Heart of Jesus, formed by the Holy Spirit in the womb of the Virgin Mother†

Heart of Jesus, substantially united to the Word of God†

Heart of Jesus, of Infinite Majesty†

Heart of Jesus, Sacred Temple of God†

Heart of Jesus, Tabernacle of the Most High†

Heart of Jesus, House of God and Gate of Heaven†

Heart of Jesus, burning furnace of charity†

Heart of Jesus, abode of justice and love†

Heart of Jesus, full of goodness and love†

Heart of Jesus, abyss of all virtues†

Heart of Jesus, most worthy of all praise†

Heart of Jesus, king and center of all hearts†

Heart of Jesus, in whom are all treasures of wisdom and knowledge†

Heart of Jesus, in whom dwells the fullness of divinity†

Heart of Jesus, in whom the Father was well pleased†

Heart of Jesus, of whose fullness we have all received†

Heart of Jesus, desire of the everlasting hills†

Heart of Jesus, patient and most merciful†

Heart of Jesus, enriching all who invoke Thee†

Heart of Jesus, fountain of life and holiness†

Heart of Jesus, propitiation for our sins†

Heart of Jesus, loaded down with opprobrium†

Heart of Jesus, bruised for our offenses†

Heart of Jesus, obedient to death†

Heart of Jesus, pierced with a lance†

Heart of Jesus, source of all consolation†

Heart of Jesus, our life and resurrection†

Heart of Jesus, our peace and our reconciliation†

Heart of Jesus, victim for our sins†

Heart of Jesus, salvation of those who trust in Thee†

Heart of Jesus, hope of those who die in Thee†

Heart of Jesus, delight of all the Saints,†

Lamb of God, Who takes away the sins of the world, *have mercy on us, Lord.*

Lamb of God, Who takes away the sins of the world, *graciously hear us, Lord.*

Lamb of God, Who takes away the sins of the world, *have mercy on us, Lord.*

V: Jesus, meek and humble of heart,

R: *Make our hearts like unto Thine.*

Chaplet of the Sacred heart of Jesus

V. O God, come to my assistance. **R.** O Lord, make haste to help me.

I. My most loving Jesus, my own heart is glad when I think upon your most Sacred Heart, all tenderness and sweetness for sinners, and I am filled with confident hope of your kind welcome. But O, my sins! how many and how great are they! Grieving now, like Peter and like Magdalene, I bewail and abhor them, because they are an offense to you, my sovereign good. O, grant me pardon for them all. Would that I might die before I offend you again! I pray by your Sacred Heart that I may live only to repay your love.

Say one Our Father, and five Glory Be's in honor of the Sacred Heart

V. Sweet Heart of my Jesus, **R.** Make me love Thee ever more and more.

II. My Jesus, I bless your most humble Heart; and I give thanks unto you, who by making it my model to not only give me strong and urgent encouragement to imitate it, but also, at the cost of so many humiliations, to grant yourself to point out, and to smooth for me the way to follow you. Cool and ungrateful that I am, how have I wandered far away from you! Pardon me, my Jesus! Take from me all hateful pride and ambition, that with lowly heart I may follow you, my Jesus, amidst humiliations, and so obtain peace and salvation. Strengthen me, you who can, and I will ever bless your Sacred Heart.

Say one Our Father, and five Glory Be's in honor of the Sacred Heart

V. Sweet Heart of my Jesus, **R.** Make me love Thee ever more and more.

III. My Jesus, I admire your most patient Heart, and I give you thanks for all the wondrous examples of unwearied patience which you have left us. It pains me that these examples still have to rebuke me for my extraordinary weakness, which shrinks from every little pain. Pour, then, into my heart, O dear Jesus, a fervent and constant love of suffering and the cross, of mortification and of penance, that following you to Calvary, I may with you attain to glory, and the joys of Paradise.

Say one Our Father, and five Glory Be's in honor of the Sacred Heart

IV. Dear Jesus, when I look first upon your most gentle Heart and then upon my own, I shudder to see how unlike mine is to yours. How I am inclined to fret and mourn when a hint, a look, or a word thwarts me! Pardon for the future all my violence; and give me grace to imitate in every contradiction your unalterable meekness, that so I may enjoy an everlasting and holy peace.

Say one Our Father, and five Glory Be's in honor of the Sacred Heart

V. Let me sing praises to Jesus for his most generous heart, the conqueror of death and hell; for well it merits every praise. I am more than ever confounded whilst I look upon my coward heart, which dreads even a rough word or injurious taunt. But it shall be so with me no more. My Jesus, I pray you for such strength that, fighting and conquering on earth, I may one day rejoice triumphantly with you in heaven.

Say one Our Father, and five Glory Be's in honor of the Sacred Heart

Let us now have recourse to Mary; and dedicating ourselves wholly to her, and trusting in her maternal heart, let us say: By all the virtue of your most sweet heart obtain for us, great Mother of God, our Mother Mary, a true and enduring devotion to the Sacred Heart of Jesus, thy Son, that, bound up in every thought and affection in union with his Heart, we may fulfill all our duties, serving our Jesus evermore with readiness of heart, and especially this day.

V. Heart of Jesus, burning with love of us,
R. Inflame our heart with love of Thee.

Let us pray: Lord, we beseech Thee, let your Holy Spirit kindle in our hearts that fire of charity which our Lord Jesus Christ, your Son, sent forth from his inmost heart upon this earth, and willed that it should be kindled exceedingly. Who lives and reigns with you in the unity of the same Holy Spirit, God forever and ever. Amen.

REPARATION OF HONOR

TO BE MADE ON THE FEAST ITSELF, OR AT ANY OTHER

O most amiable and adorable heart of Jesus! Center of all hearts, glowing with charity, and inflamed with zeal for the interest of thy Father, and the salvation of mankind! O heart ever sensible of our misery, and ever in motion to redress our evils, the real victim of love in the Holy Eucharist, and propitiatory sacrifice for sin on the altar of the cross! seeing that the generality of Christians make no other return for these thy mercies than contempt of thy favors, forgetfulness of their own obligation, and ingratitude to the best of benefactors; is it not just that we your servants, penetrated with the deepest sense of the like indignities, should enter upon a due and satisfactory reparation of honor to thy most sacred majesty? Prostrate in body and humbled in mind, before heaven and earth, we solemnly declare our utter detestation and abhorrence of such conduct. Inexpressible, we know, was the bitterness, which the multitude of our sins brought on thy tender heart; insufferable the weight of our iniquities which pressed thy face to the earth in the Garden of Olives, and unsurmountable your anguish, when expiring with love, grief, and agony on Mount Calvary, in your last breath, you would reclaim sinners to their duty and repentance. This we know, O dear Redeemer! and would most willingly redress these your sufferings by our own, or share with thee in thine.

O merciful Jesus! Ever present on our altars, and with a heart open to receive all, who labor and are burdened! O adorable Heart of Jesus, source of true contrition! Impart to our hearts the true spirit

to The Sacred Heart

of penance, and to our eyes a fountain of tears, that we may bewail and wash off our sins and those of the world. Pardon, divine Jesus, all the injuries, reproaches, and outrages done to you through the course of your holy life and bitter passion. Pardon all the impieties, irreverences, and sacrileges, which have been committed against you in the sacrament of the Eucharist from its first institution. Graciously receive the small tribute of our sincere repentance as an agreeable offering in your sight, and in requital for the benefits we daily receive from the altar, where you are a living and continual sacrifice, and in union of that bloody holocaust you presented to your eternal Father on mount Calvary from the cross.

Sweet Jesus! Give your blessing to the ardent desire we now entertain and the holy resolution we have taken, of ever loving and adoring you after a proper manner in the sacrament of love, the Eucharist, to repair by a true conversion of heart and a becoming zeal for your glory, our past negligence and infidelity. O adorable Heart who knows the clay of which we are formed, be our mediator with thy heavenly Father, whom we have so grievously offended; strengthen our weakness, confirm our resolution, and with your charity, humility, meekness, and patience, cover the multitude of our iniquities; be our support, our refuge, and our strength, that nothing else in life or death may separate us from thee.

Amen

A Prayer to the Sacred Heart of Jesus
by Saint Margaret Mary Alacoque

Lord Jesus, let my heart never rest until it finds you,
who are its center, its love, and its happiness.

By the wound in your heart pardon the sins that I
have committed whether out of malice or out of evil desires.

Place my weak heart in your own divine Heart, continually
under your protection and guidance, so that I may persevere
in doing good and in fleeing evil until my last breath.

Amen.

44

Act of Love to the Sacred Heart of Jesus
by Saint Gertrude the Great

How great, O my Jesus,

is the extent of your excessive charity! You have

prepared for me, of your most precious Body and

Blood, a divine banquet, where you give me

yourself without reserve. What has urged you to

this excess of love? Nothing but your own most

loving Heart.

O adorable Heart of my Jesus,

furnace of Divine Love, receive my soul into the

wound of your most Sacred Passion, that in this

school of charity I may learn to make a return of

love to that God who hast given me such

wonderful proofs of his love.

Amen

ADDITIONAL PRAYERS

AN OFFERING TO THE SACRED HEART OF JESUS

O DIVINE HEART OF JESUS, grant, I beseech Thee, eternal rest to the souls in Purgatory, final grace to all who are to die today, true repentance to sinners, the light of faith to pagans, your blessing to me and to all who are mine.

To you, O most loving Heart of Jesus, do I therefore commend all these souls, and for them I offer all your merits, together with the merits of the most Blessed Mother and of all the saints and angels, and also together with all the sacrifices of the Mass, the Holy Communions, the prayers and good works that are made today throughout the entire Christian world. Amen.

THE ACT OF ATONEMENT FOR SIN

MOST COMPASSIONATE HEART OF JESUS, hypostatically united Eternal Word! Ever present in the holy Eucharist, receive my homage, and the tribute of atonement for sin which I here pay, prostrate at the throne of thy justice. What have we previously been doing, my God? You have bestowed on us most notable graces, even to the surprise of heaven itself, and these without any merit on our part, even while we offended you; and as you love us beyond measure, so without measure you continually heap your blessings upon us. For all these what return have we made? What in gratitude have we not shown? O God of pity and compassion! Cast the eye of thy mercy on our present repentance, or rather look not on us; look on the blessed spirits in thy heavenly court, and especially on the ever-faithful Virgin; look on thy devout servants, who always obey your commands, hearken to your inspirations, and follow your directions. These will intercede with you in our behalf, these will atone for our sins, plead our cause, and obtain pardon for past neglects. These will keep us firm and unalterable in our present purposes and resolutions of loving and serving you more fervently hereafter. Sweet Jesus! Receive this act of atonement for sin. May it be acceptable in your sight from my hands, and those of your servants of this association, whom I particularly recommend to you. Amen

ADDITIONAL PRAYERS

THE GOLDEN ARROW

MAY THE MOST HOLY, most sacred, most adorable, most mysterious and unutterable Name of God be always praised, blessed, loved, adored and glorified in heaven, on earth and under the earth, by all the creatures of God, and by the Sacred Heart of our Lord Jesus Christ in the most Holy Sacrament of the altar.

This prayer was revealed by Our Lord to a Carmelite Nun of Tours in 1843 as a reparation for blasphemy: "This Golden Arrow will wound My Heart delightfully and heal the wounds inflicted by blasphemy." Imprimatur + T. J. Toolen, Archbishop of Mobile-Birm

MOST BOUNTIFUL HEART

MOST BOUNTIFUL HEART OF JESUS, hypostatically united to the Eternal Word. Ever present in the holy Eucharist, receive my homage, and the tribute of prayer which I here offer, prostrate at the throne of thy mercy. To whom, my God, can I address my petition with equal confidence? Your care watched over me from all eternity; in time your indulgence drew me out from my non-existence; your goodness preserves me every moment of life, and your generousness blessings feeds and nourishes me. But still, my Lord and Creator, I am surrounded with a world of enemies who continually disturb the quiet, and peace of my mind interiorly, and exteriorly assault my weakness with violence. I am tempted to cry out a thousand times in the day, "Save us, O Lord! Lest we perish!" Open then a sanctuary into which I may retire; a refuge where I may be covered again the attacks of my enemies; and harbor, where after escaping from the tempestuous waves, I may repose. You have granted the Sacred Heart of Jesus to us, and in it your servants have found these advantages. The associates of the Sacred Heart have a particular right and title to this holy and safe retreat; give them then a distinguished place in it. You, O Virgin Mother! Enforce my petition by your powerful mediation. Sweet Jesus! Receive this my prayer! May it be acceptable in your sight from my hands, and those of your servants of this association who I particularly recommend to thee. Amen

ADDITIONAL PRAYERS

THE ACT OF THANKSGIVING

MOST MAGNIFICENT HEART OF JESUS, hypostatically united to the Eternal Word! Ever present in the holy Eucharist, receive my homage and the tribute of thanksgiving which I here bring, prostrate at the throne of your bounty. In the joy of my heart I return thee thanks for all your favors. Creatures of God! Brought forth from your nothing; children of men created, redeemed and sanctified, praise and magnify your great benefactor; but chiefly you, O immaculate and most pure Virgin, preserved from all spots and blemish, enriched with the fulness of grace, exalted above the nine choirs of angels, and next in dignity to the throne of God, extol, praise, and glorify this generous dispenser of all good gifts. O most bountiful God, may thy name be ever blessed; may you be ever praised, and may your bounty be ever glorified. Sweet Jesus! Receive these my thanks. May they be acceptable in your sight from my hands, and those of your servants of this association, whom I particularly recommend to thee. Amen

TO THE SACRED HEART BY ST. FRANCIS DE SALES

May your Heart dwell always in our hearts! May your blood ever flow in the veins of our souls! O sun of our hearts, you give life to all things by the rays of your goodness! I will not go until your Heart has strengthened me, O Lord Jesus! May the Heart of Jesus be the King of my heart! Blessed be God! Amen.

MOST AMIABLE HEART

BELOVED OBJECT OF OUR MOST TENDER AFFECTIONS! May all honor, glory, love and benediction be ever given to thee. Be our comfort in adversity, our guide in prosperity, our safety in dangers, and protection against all our enemies, visible and invisible. Amen

ADDITIONAL PRAYERS

BE THOU EVER, O SACRED HEART

O SACRED HEART! May you be forever obeyed and loved by all creatures, even as man is always cherished and loved by you, you have settled your affections upon him, and with him you have ever desired to dwell. O that I could love you as you deserve and as you are loved by the angels and saints in heaven; at least with a love, if not corresponding to your favors, equal however in some measure to the greatness of the obligation I lie under. Cherubim and Seraphim! Happy citizens of the heavenly Jerusalem! And principally you, O most pure Virgin Mother! Supply by your love whatever is wanting to mine. O Jesus, may your goodness be ever praised, magnified and exalted; may you ever reign as King, Lord, and Savior over all hearts, and may your amiable heart draw all hearts to you, sweet Jesus! Receive this act of love. May it be acceptable in your sight from my hand, and those of your servants of this association, whom I particularly recommend to you. Amen.

PRAYER FOR DAILY NEGLECTS

A Poor Clare nun, who had just died, appeared to her abbess, who was praying for her, and said to her, "I went straight to heaven, for, by means of this prayer, recited every evening, I paid my debts." **This prayer is not meant to replace the Sacrament of Reconciliation.**

ETERNAL FATHER, I offer you the Sacred Heart of Jesus, with all its love, all its sufferings and all its merits.

First: To expiate all the sins I have committed this day and during all my life. *Glory be to the Father and to the Son...*

Second: To purify the good I have done badly this day and during all my life. *Glory be to the Father and to the Son...*

Third: To supply for the good I ought to have done and that I have neglected this day and during all my life. *Glory be to the Father and to the Son...*

ADDITIONAL PRAYERS

INFLAME OUR HEARTS

O HEART OF JESUS, burning with love of us, inflame our hearts with the love of you. Blessed be the most adorable Heart of Jesus my God forever and ever. No love, no heart equals yours, most loving Jesus. O may your adorable Heart be forever praised, and all thanks both in time and eternity paid to it. O adorable Heart of Jesus! May you be known, loved, and adored throughout the whole world. O divine Heart, ever burning and never ceasing, raise my heart into a flame, that I may always love, and never cease from loving thee. Amen.

PRAYER FOR REPARATION OF THE SACRED HEART

All the faithful adorers of Jesus are invited to repair in spirit every day, at nine o'clock in the morning and also in the evening, to his divine heart, in order to make in common some of the following aspirations.

O MOST SACRED HEART OF JESUS, have mercy on us. O divine Heart, wounded for love of us! Let us ever be sensible of your bounty, and let your love ever plead in our favor. Amen.

PRAYER TO THE HOST HOLY SACRAMENT AND TO THE SACRED HEART OF JESUS

BEHOLD, MY MOST LOVING JESUS, to what an excess your boundless love has carried you. Of your own flesh and Precious Blood you have made ready for me a banquet in order to give me all yourself. What was it that impelled you to this transport of love for me? It was your Heart, your loving Heart. O adorable Heart of my Jesus, burning furnace of Divine Love! Within your most sacred wound receive my soul; that in this school of charity I may learn to return the love of that God who has given me such wondrous proofs of his love. Amen.

ADDITIONAL PRAYERS

THE SACRED HEART PRAYER

O **SACRED HEART OF JESUS,** living and life giving fountain of eternal life, infinite treasury of the divinity, and glowing furnace of love, you are my refuge and my sanctuary. O adorable and glorious Savior, consume my heart with that burning fire that ever inflames your Heart.

Pour down on my souls those graces that flow from your love. Let my heart be so united with yours that our wills may be one, and mine may in all things be conformed to yours. May your will be the rule of both my desires and my actions. Amen.

This prayer is thought to be originally prayed by St. Gertrude and adapted by St. Alphonse Liguori; he is considered the author because of its final formulation.

ADDITIONAL PRAYERS

ADDITIONAL PRAYERS

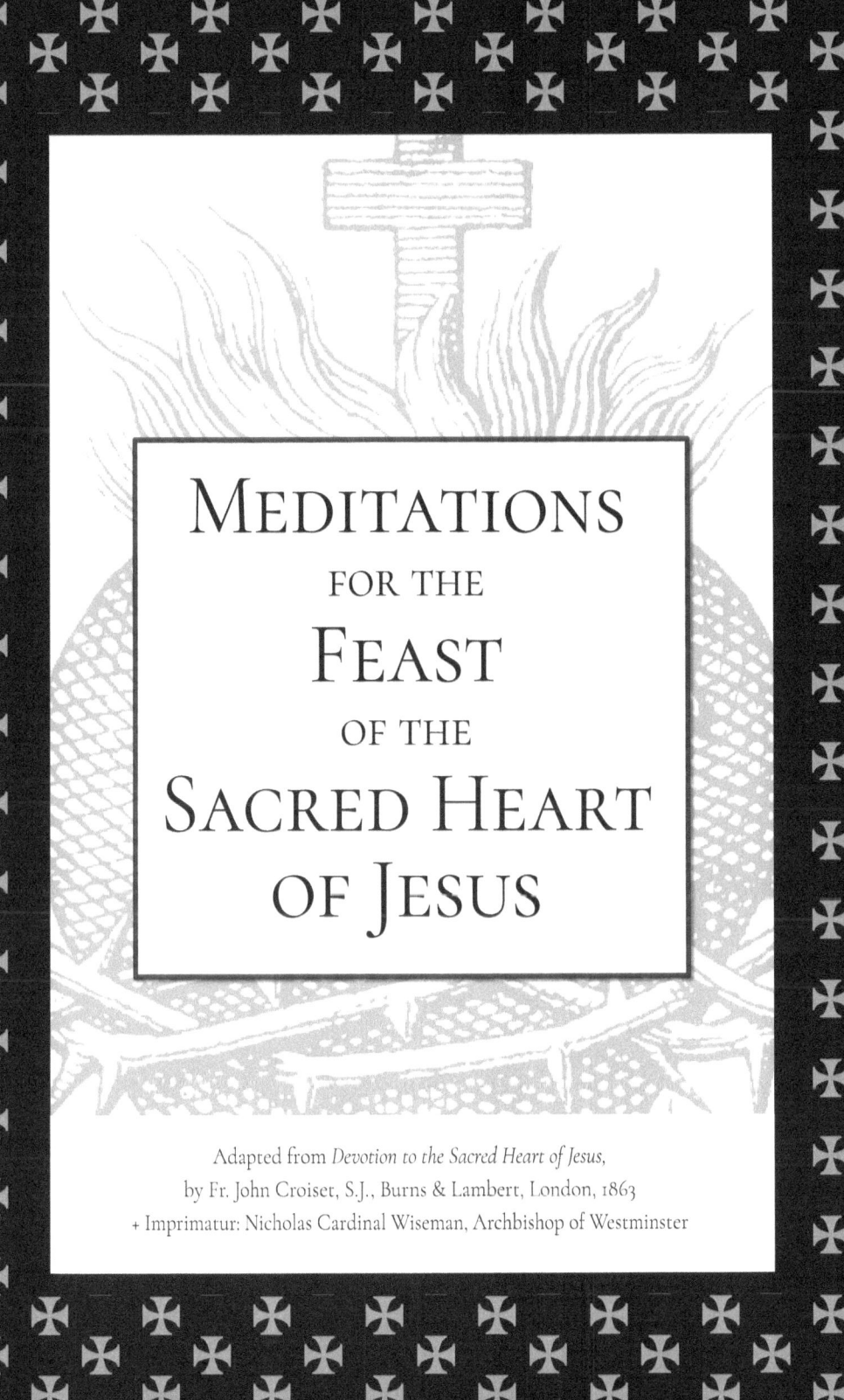

Meditations
for the
Feast
of the
Sacred Heart
of Jesus

Adapted from *Devotion to the Sacred Heart of Jesus,*
by Fr. John Croiset, S.J., Burns & Lambert, London, 1863
+ Imprimatur: Nicholas Cardinal Wiseman, Archbishop of Westminster

For each Friday of the month, and for certain days of the year, more especially consecrated to the honor of the Sacred Heart of our Lord Jesus Christ.

The two Meditations that follow have been given at length, to facilitate their use by all sorts of persons, and by those also, who say they do not know how to meditate. I ask these last, only to read them with attention, reflecting on what they have read, and I hope that they will find that this reading has not been altogether useless, since, when accompanied with the affectionate sentiments towards Jesus Christ, with which grace will not fail to inspire our hearts, it will be a true prayer. Those to whom the habit of prayer is familiar, can content themselves with looking over the subject of each point.

MEDITATION FOR THE FIRST FRIDAY AFTER THE OCTAVE OF CORPUS CHRISTI

On the incomprehensible love shown us by Jesus Christ in the most Blessed Sacrament of the Altar.

The subject of this Meditation is the incomprehensible love shown us by Jesus Christ in the adorable Sacrament of the altar, where he is so little known to men, and still less loved, even by those to whom he is known.

The end that we should propose to ourselves in this meditation, and which should be its fruit, is to have a most lively feeling of the extreme ingratitude of men, the greater part of whom are insensible to the evident marks of this ardent love, in order to repair, by a return of love, by our adorations, and by every kind of homage all the insults that the adorable Heart of Jesus Christ has received, until now, in the most Blessed Sacrament.

The subject of the three points may be taken from three motives, or three desires of Jesus Christ, in the institution of this mystery.

1. The excessive desire that Jesus Christ has had to be always with us.
2. The desire he has to make us partakers of all his benefits.
3. The desire he has to be closely united to us, though men are insensible to the proofs of so ardent a love.

PRELUDE: We may represent to ourselves the upper-chamber in which the Son of God, seated in the midst of his disciples, instituted this adorable mystery, the contempt to which he exposed himself, even at that time, in communicating, the traitor Judas, not being able to deter him for a single moment, from the institution of this mystery of love.

Convinced, by an act of faith, of the truth of this adorable mystery, and disposed, by an act of contrition, to receive the lights and graces, which God is ready to grant on this occasion, let us ask of the Holy Ghost, in the name of Jesus Christ himself, and through the intercession of the Blessed Virgin, and of our Guardian Angel, the grace to conceive a great sorrow for so much contempt and ingratitude, penetrating deeply into the loving sentiments of the Heart of Jesus Christ in the Blessed Sacrament.

First Point: The ardent desire Jesus Christ feels to be with us.

Consider that the Sacred Heart of Jesus Christ was no sooner formed within the womb of the Blessed Virgin, than it was inflamed with an immense love for all men; but, as it is the property of love, to desire to be continually with those, for whom this love is felt, a life of thirty-three years appeared to him too short to satisfy his excessive desire of being continually with us. It was necessary to work the greatest of miracles, to content the greatest of all desires. This Heart could not place limits to the excess of its love. Be not afflicted, oh my apostles, said our loving Jesus, if I am obliged to leave you to ascend to Heaven; my Heart desires with more ardor to be with you, than you desire to be with me, and as long as there are men upon earth I shall be with them. All the motives that led the Son of God to clothe himself with our flesh have ceased. The work of redemption is fulfilled. Nothing but his excessive desire of being continually with us, obliges him to work this constant miracle, and this compendium of all his wonders; his immense love making it, as it were, impossible to him to be separated from us. Jesus has ascended to his Father: why does he every day return invisibly on earth, if not because he cannot separate himself from men, and his delights are to be with us? Who would ever have thought that Jesus Christ could have loved us to this excess? From the greatest height of glory he desires to come and dwell in our hearts, as if something were wanting to his felicity, when he is at a distance from us. A desire must be very violent, when it cannot be satisfied in Heaven, where all desires are fulfilled. Jesus Christ must love men passionately, since not restrained, by the great glory he has enjoyed since his ascension, he every day places himself, in a humble and obscure state on our altars, to satisfy the excess of his love and of his tenderness; proving to us the truth of what he had said by his Prophet, that his delights are to be with us.

REFLECTIONS

1. These are the tender sentiments, with which the love that inflames his Sacred Heart, inspires Jesus Christ; but what must be his sentiments, seeing the forgetfulness and indifference of those, whom he loves to such an excess, and who love him so little?

2. Jesus Christ has no need of men, and yet he loves them to such a degree, that he counts it as nothing, to be shut up within a host, until the end of ages, for the sake of the pleasure he has in being with us. Men, on the contrary, cannot do without Jesus Christ, and yet they love him so little, that they think nothing of this prodigy, so little do they value the joy of conversing with him.

3. What were the sentiments of Jesus Christ, when he saw himself abandoned by a whole people, whom he had loaded with benefits, and even by his most zealous disciples? What must be the sentiments of this blessed Savior in the adorable Sacrament of the altar, where, for the greater part of the day, he is forsaken by all, and where perhaps so many religious persons, who possess him in their own house, visit him so rarely?

4. Jesus Christ dwells corporally amongst us, and there is no concourse in the places where he resides. All the places of amusement, all the public squares are full of people. There is always a crowd in the palaces of the great; time is always found for visiting them, though they are scarcely ever in so amiable a mood as to be pleased with the services rendered them; while Jesus Christ is left alone in the churches, though he never refuses any one, and receives with exceeding mildness and joy all who approach him. he says, complaining by the mouth of his prophet, "I am left alone in my churches, and no one can find half a quarter of an hour, to honor me in the Blessed Sacrament of the altar."

5. Visits among men are so ordinary and so frequent; it is only this loving Jesus who is not visited.

6. If sweetness in conversation or interest attracts us, what conversation is there sweeter or more useful than that which we have with the most amiable and most powerful person in the world, and who loves us more than any other? His conversation has neither sadness nor weariness; those chosen souls give testimony of it, who are always immersed in sweetness in his presence, and who would willingly pass whole days and nights at the foot of his altars.

7. Beloved Jesus, what must be the sentiments of your Heart, seeing the insensibility and the ingratitude Of man? You offer yourself for them many times every day in sacrifice on our altars, and one half hour spent in this solemn offering seems to them too long; they are compelled to relieve their weariness and the annoyance they feel by continual distractions of mind.

8. Ungrateful men! You do not know him who continually dwells in the midst of you. If we do not know Jesus Christ, we are lost without remedy, for eternal life consists in knowing him. But what hope can there be, if when we know him, we do not love him?

9. Can we say that we love him? Should we be satisfied, if he loved us no more than we love him? Should we not desire to be better loved by men than we ourselves love Jesus Christ? Would it be sufficient if our friends showed us no more affection than we evince towards this loving Savior? Should we desire that persons, whom we think we have obliged, should feel for us the same gratitude we show him? And should we allow our children and our servants, to be as little respectful in our presence, as we are, in the presence of Jesus Christ in his churches, at the foot of his altars? My God, the angels surround these altars in crowds, to adore and love this adorable Jesus, though he is not in the Blessed Sacrament for them. Men, for whom alone he has wrought this miracle, do not condescend to visit him.

Lord! Who, to satisfy your excessive desire of being with me, has invented this miracle, what sentiments have you of the forgetfulness I have shown towards you until now? Is this my correspondence with your love? There is no man whom, if he had the least goodwill towards me, I should not have visited more willingly and more frequently. There is no creature that I should not have loved more. I have forgotten you, oh Lord, and until now I have not loved you; what can I expect, ungrateful and unfaithful as I am, that you should think of me? And when have you ever ceased to do it? Have I not reason to expect that my wanderings, my insensibility, my forgetfulness, and my ingratitude, might oblige you to think of me no more. Ah, my beloved Savior, remember this. I have given you so many reasons for forgetting me, for despising me, and for only remembering me, in order to cast me into hell. You have not done it. God of goodness, I thank you, and in future I desire to serve you better. I humbly ask pardon of you for my ingratitude towards you. I hope that, by your grace, I shall repair in future, by my assiduity in visiting you, in this adorable mystery, the loss I have sustained by my indifference; and that if your temple is not my usual habitation, I shall at least have a secure refuge in your adorable Heart, which I choose at this moment for my habitation, and which I desire no more to quit.

Second Point: The excessive desire of Jesus Christ to make us partakers of his blessings.

Consider, that as Jesus Christ is the source of all goods, he wished to dwell among us, only to be ready at all times to make us partakers of his treasures. And this loving Savior has not only desired to make us, in this adorable Sacrament, partakers of all the blessings of which he is the source, but he has willed, in giving himself, to give us the very fountain of all blessings. I will bestow on you all sorts of benefits, but where else can you find all sorts of blessings upon earth, except in the most blessed Sacrament? The princes of the earth display their liberality, only at certain times, and to certain persons. Jesus Christ, in the Blessed Sacrament, gives all, at all times, and to all persons. It might be said, that we must be poor and afflicted, to have a right to draw near to this fountain of every good, and of all graces: that it suffices to be unhappy to be well received. This God of goodness, foreseeing our weakness and our infirmities, gives himself to us, for food to repair our strength, and to be a sovereign remedy against all our evils. Why do you weep, says this loving Savior continually to us, and why are you grieved at the loss of your health, of your children, or of your property? Do you not find in me all these goods, and even more? It did not satisfy the love our divine Savior bears us, only to open to us his divine Heart, and to pour on us his blessings and graces. He desires to be also our strength and our shield, against all the efforts of our mortal enemies. Lastly, what more could Jesus Christ give us? What present could he make us, that he has not made, in giving himself to us?

REFLECTIONS

1. This divine Savior comes to us full of goodness, of love, and of the most ardent love, and we go to him daily, with coldness and indifference. He comes to us, loaded with graces and treasures to enrich us, and how long shall we go to him, with our hands empty of good works, and with our hearts so filled with the love of creatures, that they cannot have any share in the great liberality of this divine Savior?

2. There is no blessing which Jesus Christ has not given us, in giving himself in the blessed Eucharist; and there is no irreverence, no outrage, that has not been offered to Jesus Christ in this august Sacrament.

3. He is despised only because he has done us too much good, because he has loved us too much.

4. The house and the person, of the vilest and most wicked of men, would have been treated with more respect, than his temples and his sacred Body have received.

5. Love has obliged Jesus Christ to conceal himself, to come down upon our altars, but to what does he expose himself, by coming thus disguised? How much contempt, how many insults is he obliged to endure daily, from bad Christians, and from infidels. How many licentious men, how many heretics treat him on our altars, as if he were a mock divinity, renewing all the outrages that he suffered in his Passion, on account of the royalty to which he laid claim.

6. The Jews exercised less cruelty towards his person than is exercised daily towards his sacred Body. The consecrated hosts have been trodden under foot, they have been pierced with a thousand blows, they have been broken in pieces and burnt; without speaking of the terrible uses to which they have been put, and which we cannot think of without horror.

7. The choice which Jesus Christ had made of the insults and outrages he received in Jerusalem, took away their bitterness; but who would dare to think that this Heart, which has only placed itself in this condition to be more loved and honored by men, could regard with indulgence the extraordinary contempt that is shown him?

8. We feel compassion for a man that is despised and ill-treated. Jesus Christ is the only one to whose outrages we are insensible; it even seems as if every one took pleasure in ill-treating him.

9. We make a child keep silence, if it cries or makes a noise, in the house of a person of quality, whom we are visiting, and we accustom it, by a sinful indulgence, to be ill-behaved in the Church, as soon as it can walk. We stand in Church, we laugh, we talk without restraint, even during the holy Sacrifice. We are more modest in a place of amusement: we are more attentive at a play, than at the celebration of these adorable mysteries. Young men carry their insolence to the foot of the altar, and even glory in it, while the Turks do not dare to raise their eyes in their mosques, in which to laugh or talk would be a crime punishable with death.

10. How many houses in these times, are most richly furnished! How many persons would be ashamed to wear the shabby ornaments, on which the Body of Jesus Christ reposes!

11. What answer could we make to heretics, if in reproving us for our immodesty in Church, they boasted of being more religious than we? If you believe that Jesus Christ is on that altar in that host, you who understand so well the rules of propriety and of civility, you who are so guarded, I do not say in the palaces and antechambers of the great, but in the houses. of your friends, if you believe, how comes it that you lose so completely all respect for your God? "We have nothing but contempt for your sacraments," might a heretic say to us, "but do you not yourselves teach us to despise them?"

12. It cannot be denied that the Gentiles treated with respect, even the most profane ceremonies. Christians have the most holy of all mysteries and they do not cease to profane them! Which merit the severer judgment?

those who have been religious even to superstition, or those who have been impious even to sacrilege? And have we not reason to fear, that these infidels will one day be our accusers?

13. All agree that this is the most enormous of all acts of ingratitude: we feel horror when we think of it, and yet we are witnesses of all this impiety; sometimes perhaps we have authority over those who are guilty of it, and we allow it, and are insensible to this forgetfulness, this indifference, these outrages, these profanations, these sacrileges?

14. Jesus Christ, always full of compassion for our miseries, is continually despised, outraged, and profaned by all sorts of persons, and who troubles himself about it, or has any feeling of it?

Oh hardness! Oh insensibility of the hearts of men! Oh most adorable and most amiable Heart of my beloved Jesus! Heart worthy of the respect and adorations of men and angels: Heart truly worthy to possess all hearts, to reign over all hearts; what must be your sentiments at the sight of so many outrages? But, what ought to be the sentiments of my heart, seeing you so ill-treated? You see Lord what feeling I have of all these indignities. Humbly prostrate here before you, I make a reparation to your honor, and I humbly ask pardon for them. Why cannot I in some measure, repair so many outrages that have been committed, or at least prevent others from being offered you. But, my beloved Savior, all my desires are useless, if I were to shed all my blood I could not hinder either one or the other, but at least I have a heart capable of loving you, capable of offering you homage; and this, my Savior, is what consoles me. I have a heart, and this heart shall love you, and shall love nothing in the future but you. I offer you, with this heart, all the desires and emotions of which it is capable. I offer you, oh my Savior, all that I can do, aided by your grace; all that can please you, all that can honor you. I invite and humbly beseech all the angels, all the Blessed, and also your own Blessed Mother to supply for my weakness and my desires. I beg them to honor you, praise you, adore you, and love you for me, and for all men. Permit me, in order to honor you worthily, to offer you yourself: for I may say that you art mine, and that in future all your desires shall be mine. I will praise you, oh beloved Jesus, and I will publish everywhere, that you alone ought to be loved, served, praised, and honored eternally.

Third Point: The excessive desire of Jesus Christ to he united with us.

Consider that the union of hearts is the uttermost effect of love: and yet this has been the intention of Jesus Christ, in instituting this august Sacrament, in which all his actions are those of a passionate lover of men; for in this Sacrament love makes him, as it were, go out of himself, to live no more but in the beloved object. This Sacrament is a mystery of union. It is true that by the incarnation, Almighty God has united himself perfectly to our nature; but this hypostatic union was not the end of his incarnation, as the sacramental union was the end of the institution of the Blessed Sacrament. He united himself to our nature, to have a body capable of the sufferings he desired to endure for us; but he gives himself to us in the Eucharist, only to unite himself intimately to us. He invites us to this banquet by his promises. He induces us to go by his threats. He commands that we should be made to enter as it were by force.

Lastly, he does everything to inflame us with a great desire of going to him, that there may be nothing to oppose that which possesses him of coming to us and being closely united with us. Was there ever a stronger proof of a most ardent love? How is it Lord? Have you forgotten the bad treatment you received among us? Or have you not foreseen that, to which the excess of your love for us exposes you? The heart of a chaste and fervent person is an agreeable dwelling for you, but how many will you find? Can you endure the coldness of the number of slothful Christians that receive you with their contempt, their want of faith, and above all, the frightful corruption of their hearts? These are great obstacles, especially for a Heart that cannot endure anything defiled: but the strength of his love overcomes everything. Conceive, if possible, the hatred God bears to sin: it is infinite: and yet, in a certain manner, it is less than the desire he has of coming to us, for he prefers to give himself up, so to speak, to the sacrilegious embraces of the most infamous sinners, rather than renounce the delight he feels in being closely united with those who love him. See to what an excess our Savior loves us in this adorable mystery, that a God should deign to be himself our reward. What a wonder that Jesus Christ should be himself our food! This is a miracle of love that surpasses our comprehension: it is a liberality in which, so to speak, Jesus Christ has exhausted himself. These are the effects of the tenderness and of the immense love of our Blessed Savior.

REFLECTIONS

1. We believe this miracle: and we are insensible to this excess of love.

2. It is surprising that our Lord can love men to this extent: but it is most extraordinary that men should not love this divine Savior, and that no motive, no benefit, no excess of love, can inspire us with the least feeling of gratitude!

3. Ungrateful man! Insensible man! What do you see in him, that keeps you at a distance? Has he not done enough to merit our love? Alas! he has done more than we should have dared to wish for, more than we can believe, more in a certain way than was becoming his infinite Majesty, and shall we still remain in doubt, whether we will correspond with so great generosity or whether we shall continue to despise it?

4. A mark of affection, a service rendered, gains the hearts of men; Jesus Christ alone, who, after exhausting himself in this mystery of love, after giving himself to men, does not gain their hearts.

5. All agree that Jesus Christ loves us infinitely, that he is infinitely worthy of love, that he has, besides, done all that can be imagined to make himself loved by men. Yet very few love Jesus Christ in reality.

6. When is it that he desires so eagerly to come to us, and that we must be constrained to go to him? Because he loves us passionately, and we do not love him at all.

7. When is it that we depart from communion quite frozen, though we have been nourished with the Sacred Heart of Jesus Christ, which is all fire, all love? Because we approach with a heart full of creatures, with a closed heart, impenetrable to the darts of his love. Because his Heart indeed enters into ours, but ours does not enter into his, because we have a sort of dislike to enter there.

8. We prefer to give up communion rather than our vices. We should be obliged to be more circumspect, to love Jesus Christ more, to lead a more regular life, if we received more often this bread of angels. The love of

Jesus Christ is inconvenient to us: we prefer to abstain longer from this bread of life, and even to condemn frequent communion, because our heart feels an excessive disgust for the Body and even for the Heart of Jesus Christ.

9. Might Jesus Christ now say to us: I desire with ardor, with eagerness, to unite myself closely to you! And how is it, that nothing is neglected to render these desires inefficacious which so well merit universal gratitude?

10. Jesus Christ desires to come to us frequently, well knowing that this is the only means of rendering us daily less unworthy of it: and there are Christians, who under the pretext that they are not worthy, render themselves daily more unworthy by withdrawing from Jesus Christ.

11. If this were a true sentiment of humility, they would most certainly possess the virtue that render us most worthy: but it is only disgust, for the Body of Jesus Christ that keeps them at a distance, and even makes them blame those who approach more frequently.

12. The apparent humility of St. Peter, which led him to refuse to allow Jesus Christ to wash his feet, was so strongly condemned, that he would have been irremediably lost, if he had not changed his conduct. How many, through a pretended respect, through false modesty, keep away from life, and are lost without remedy, by abstaining from holy communion.

13. The Gentiles and the barbarous nations of the East cried out, on only hearing of this mystery: What a good God is the God of the Christians! What a benefactor! He is most worthy of love! But, what would they have thought, had they been told that this loving God was scarcely loved at all by Christians, that this exquisite food had no attraction for them, and that on the contrary, they had a disgust for it, and that they made use of the humble and obscure state to which the excess of his love has reduced him, to commit the greatest sacrileges and the most execrable profanations.

14. What must be the sentiments of the Sacred Heart of Jesus, the source of all purity, when he is, as it were, buried in a heart full of filth, in a heart which breathes nothing but hatred, revenge, and imprecations against the Savior whom it receives? But what ought to be ours, knowing with

what malice this innocent lamb is treated, who opens not his mouth amidst so many insults and outrages, who allows himself to be led to the altar, who allows himself to be sacrificed for our salvation?

15. Will such excessive goodness, so great meekness, never have power to touch us? It softened the heart of his judge; it changed into respect and love the insolence and rage of his executioners; it has softened the hardness of the hearts, of the most barbarous people: shall there be no hearts but ours, that it cannot move?

16. Every one shudders with horror at the mere recital of the treason of Judas, or of the rage of the Jews; we are daily witnesses, and perhaps accomplices, in the sacrileges and outrages, that are offered to our loving Jesus, in this adorable mystery, and we are not touched by them.

17. "You have before your eyes those who so ill-treat me in this sacrament of love," says he to us by the mouth of his prophet; "you are a witness of their irreverence. My Heart exposed to so many indignities, bears them with patience. I thought there would be someone at least to take part in my griefs, I have waited until now, and no one presents himself; I expected that someone would try to repair by his love, his adorations, and his homage, the indignities with which my Heart is afflicted, and the contempt that is shown for my love, and I have not found any one."

No, no, Lord: it shall never be true that you are abandoned; I will put an end to these just complaints. Oh my loving Savior, is this the way in which we correspond with your love? Why have you loved us so much? But rather, why do we love you so little? Why do we not love you at all? I have not been satisfied with insensibility to the love and tender sentiments of your Heart; with insensibility to the outrages that have been committed against you. I have been myself of the number of those who have thus insulted you. My loving Savior, whose Heart is always burning with love for me, always open to reserve me, always ready to show me mercy, pardon me my former forgetfulness of you, pardon me my tepidity, my want of faith, my irreverence, and receive the act of reparation that I here make for you, prostrate before you. You think of me continually in this august Sacrament, You love me continually, you have only sentiments of tenderness for me; and shall I forget you, O Lord? And shall I feel only indifference for you? And shall I not love you, O my God? Take me out of life if I am to continue to love you so little. Let my heart be annihilated if it is to be in the future insensible to the greatest of all benefits, that is, towards you, O my God, who, in giving yourself to us, has given us the most precious present, and the most choice favor you could bestow.

Oh Christian, what the Lord asks of thee: He asks thee to love him; he only asks thy heart. What can it be that I oblige you to beg for my heart, after you have given me yours, that I should make you ask for this heart, and even refuse it, though I daily give it lavishly to creatures? Ah my loving Jesus, if I offer it now, will you accept it? This heart is contrite, it is humble; it cannot fail to please you, O Lord. Receive then this heart, which I offer with all the movements of which it is capable, to honor you and love you, all the rest of my life. The greater number of the years of my life are past and gone, and are lost, because I did not love you, but the happiest are left, because I will love you in the future: I will love you, oh adorable Heart of my beloved Jesus; I will love you, oh Sacred Heart, wounded in the Eucharist by the love of me. I will honor you during the rest of my life; you shalt be my repose, my constant abode, and my place of refuge. Let no one seek me elsewhere; I will in the future be found no more but in the Heart of my loving Jesus. This Sacred Heart is the place of my abode; this Heart shall be my food. In it I will rest from all my labors, burning with the same fire of love with which it burns, with it and in it I will love him.

The Meditation may be concluded with the following:

Anima Christi

Soul of Christ, sanctify me.
Body of Christ, save me.
Blood of Christ, inebriate me.
Water from the side of Christ, wash me.
Passion of Christ, strengthen me.
O good Jesus, hear me.
Within your wounds conceal me.
Do not permit me to be parted from you.
From the evil foe protect me.
At the hour of my death call me.
And bid me come to you,
to praise you with all your saints
for ever and ever.
Amen.

Our Lord Jesus Christ desires that we should,
for sanctifying ourselves,
glorify his all-loving heart;
for it was his heart that suffered the most
in his sacred humanity.

Saint Margaret Mary Alacoque

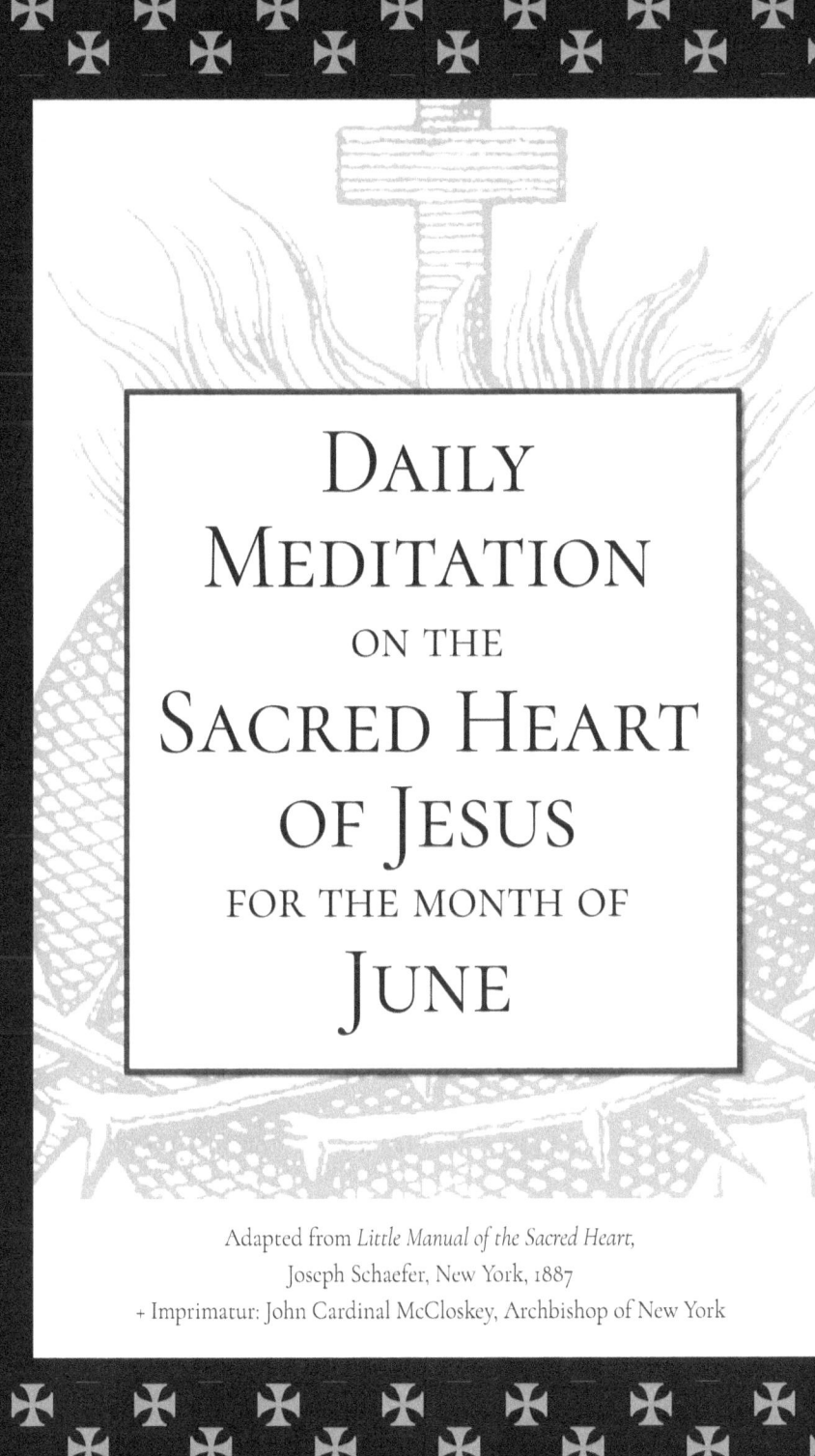

DAILY
MEDITATION
ON THE
SACRED HEART
OF JESUS
FOR THE MONTH OF
JUNE

Adapted from *Little Manual of the Sacred Heart*,
Joseph Schaefer, New York, 1887
+ Imprimatur: John Cardinal McCloskey, Archbishop of New York

A Devout Aspiration To The Sacred Heart

Most amiable Heart of Jesus: beloved object of our most tender affections! May all honor, glory, love and benediction be ever given to you. Be our comfort in adversity, our guide in prosperity, our safety in dangers, and protection against all our enemies, visible and invisible. Amen

Offering Of The Month

O Sacred Heart of Jesus, source of every grace, virtue, and benediction, moved by that tender mercy of thine, which has so loved me even when I loved thee not; I hope that now when I really do desire to love and serve thee, thou wilt still love and bless me. Accept, O most injured and divine Heart, my desire of consecrating this month to thy special honor and imitation, and in reparation for the insults and neglect thou received the greatest pledge of thy Heart's love, the Holy Sacrament of the altar. I offer you my body, my health, my labors, my life, my soul, my heart, and all that I have or am, to be employed purely for thy love. In giving thee my heart, through the heart of thy Sacred Mother, I give you but little, but it is all I have, and all that you desire. Take, then, my heart, change it, cover it and purify it and make it entirely yours. Amen.

General Protectors for the month: Mary and Joseph, the first and truest adorers of the Sacred Heart of Jesus.

June 1ˢᵗ — The Sacred Heart Of Jesus, The Center Of All Hearts

Protectors for this day: The Holy Angels, and St. Joachim and St. Anne

PRACTICE: Begin this month well. Offer yourself with Jesus and to Jesus, at the offertory of the Holy Mass. Make the Act of Consecration to the Sacred Heart (pg. 27). *Recite the Aspiration on pg. 72*

Prayer: Sacred Heart of Jesus, I give myself wholly to thee.

June 2ⁿᵈ — The Sacred Heart Of Jesus, Our Victim

Protectors for this day: The Archangels, and St. John, the Disciple of love

PRACTICE: At the Holy Sacrifice this day, offer yourself as a victim, in union with the Sacred Heart of Jesus, and make the Act of Reparation (pg. 42) to this Blessed Victim for your sins, especially: do this with fervor and sincerity at the Offertory. *Recite the Aspiration on pg. 72*

Prayer: Sacred Heart of Jesus, Victim of my sins, mercy! mercy!

June 3ʳᵈ — The Sacred Heart Of Jesus, Our Ransom

Protectors for this day: The Thrones, and St. Bonaventure

PRACTICE: Full reparation for any scandal or bad example you may have previously given. Try to ransom some poor soul from Purgatory, and labor and pray for the conversion of sinners. Have a Mass offered for these intentions, or assist at Mass as a true child of God. *Recite the Aspiration on pg. 72*

Prayer: "Shall I not live and die for him, who has lived and died for me."
— St. Francis DeSales

June 4th — *The Sacred Heart Of Jesus, Penitent for Our Sins*

Protectors for this day: The Angel Gabriel, and Sts. Peter, James, and John

PRACTICE: Make your confession in union with the penitent Heart of Jesus in Gethsemane. Beg of Jesus to give you a share of that sorrow which he felt in the Garden of Olives, for those sins of which you are going to accuse yourself. *Recite the Aspiration on pg. 72*

Prayer: "Not my will, but Thine, be done." O! Sacred Heart of Jesus! Pardon! Mercy! Conversion!

June 5th — *The Sacred Heart Of Jesus, Our Sacrifice*

Protectors for this day: The Dominions, and St. Mary Magdalene

PRACTICE: Assist at Mass today, in union with the Holy Virgin Mother, the beloved Disciple, and the grateful & penitent Magdalene at the foot of the Cross, in the full spirit of sacrifice. Give up all that the Sacred Heart requires. Ask all that you wish with strong faith and unbounded confidence. Say the Litany of the Sacred Heart (pg. 39). *Recite the Aspiration on pg. 72*

Prayer: Heart of Jesus, made obedient even to the death of the Cross, have mercy on me!

June 6th — *The Sacred Heart Of Jesus, The Author And Finisher Of Our Faith*

Protectors for this day: The Powers, and St. Thomas the Apostle

PRACTICE: In the spirit of lively faith, say the Nicene or Apostles' Creed. Kiss often the image of the Sacred Heart, begging lively faith, working by the charity of this loving heart. Show the world our faith by your entire conduct. *Recite the Aspiration on pg. 72*

Prayer: Sacred Heart of Jesus, give me a lively and strong faith!

June 7th — *The Sacred Heart Of Jesus, Our Hope*

Protectors for this day: The Principalities, and St. Augustine

PRACTICE: Perform all your actions this day, in the spirit of hope and confidence in the Sacred Heart of Jesus. Say the "Magnificat" to beg the virtue of hope. *Recite the Aspiration on pg. 72*

Prayer: Sacred Heart of Jesus, in you I will hope!

June 8th — *The Sacred Heart Of Jesus, Our Light*

Protectors for this day: The Virtues, and St. Teresa

PRACTICE: With all the fervor of your soul say a prayer to the Holy Spirit, earnestly begging light and strength to know and do God's will, according to your vocation. Resolve to be faithful to the particular Examen. *Recite the Aspiration on pg. 72*

Prayer: Lord, that I may see.

The Magnificat

My soul proclaims the greatness of the Lord, my spirit rejoices in God my Savior. For he has looked with favor on his lowly servant. From this day all generations will call me blessed: the Almighty has done great things for me, and holy is his Name. He has mercy on those who fear him in every generation. He has shown the strength of his arm, he has scattered the proud in their conceit. He has cast down the mighty from their thrones, and has lifted up the lowly. He has filled the hungry with good things, and the rich he has sent away empty. He has come to the help of his servant Israel for he remembered his promise of mercy, the promise he made to our fathers, to Abraham and his children forever.

June 9th — *The Sacred Heart Of Jesus, Our Strength*

Protectors for this day: The Cherubim, and St. Bernard

PRACTICE: Renounce, this day, before the image of the Sacred Heart of Jesus, all trust in yourself and creatures. Say fervently the Act of Consecration (pg. 27), to beg the grace to begin, to do, and to suffer all things in this great and powerful Heart. *Recite the Aspiration on pg. 72*

Prayer: Sacred, Omnipotent, Heart of Jesus, strengthen me in this hour.

June 10th — *The Sacred Heart Of Jesus, The Way, The Truth, And The Life*

Protectors for this day: The Seraphim, and the Angels of the Association of St. Francis de Sales

PRACTICE: Earnestly beg this day, true devotion to the Sacred Heart of Jesus, "the Way, the Truth and the Life." Pray for it every time the clock strikes in a fervent elevation of the heart, and beg it through Mary and Joseph, the first lovers of this Divine Heart. *Recite the Aspiration on pg. 72*

Prayer: Sacred Heart of Jesus, our "Way, Truth, and Life," help me to know, love, and imitate you.

June 11th — *The Sacred Heart Of Jesus, Our King*

Protectors for this day: The Holy Guardian Angels, St. Ignatius, and all the Saints of his Society

PRACTICE: Consecrate yourself with all the fervor of your soul, as did St. Ignatius to the Sacred Heart of Jesus, your glorious King and Captain. Often say with fervor the "Our Father," dwelling on the words "Thy Kingdom come." *Recite the Aspiration on pg. 72*

Prayer: Live, Jesus our King, and Mary our Queen.

June 12ᵗʰ — *The Sacred Heart Of Jesus, Our Master*

Protectors for this day: The Holy Angels of those who announce the word of God, and Sts. Xavier and Regis

PRACTICE: Say the Litany of St. Aloysius (pg. 78), and beg of him to obtain for you and your family true devotion to the Sacred Heart. On this day the Novena of St. Aloysius commences. *Recite the Aspiration on pg. 72*

Prayer: Master, I will follow thee whither so ever thou goes.

June 13ᵗʰ — *The Sacred Heart Of Jesus, Our School*

Protectors for this day: The Holy Angels of our friends, and St. Thomas de Pazzi

PRACTICE: Take up in earnest the challenge of a Father of the Society of Jesus: "Go on trial to the School of the Sacred Heart of Jesus for fourteen days, and if at the end of this time you perceive no improvement in your soul, I give you leave to go elsewhere." Say the Litany of the Sacred Heart (pg. 39), to beg meekness and humility. *Recite the Aspiration on pg. 72*

Prayer: Sacred Heart of Jesus, meek and humble, teach me thy own favorite lesson.

June 14ᵗʰ — *The Sacred Heart Of Jesus, Our Book*

Protectors for this day: St. Michael the Archangel, and St Gertrude

PRACTICE: For this day, spend a quarter of an hour reading the living book of the Sacred Heart of Jesus, if possible before the Blessed Sacrament, and beg Mary and Joseph to open for you. Perhaps the first words will be "Learn of me for I am Meek and Humble," or "Child give me thy heart." Make an act of faith before the Blessed Sacrament. *Recite the Aspiration on pg. 72*

Prayer: Mary, my true mother, open to me and teach me to read, understand, and practice the book of life, the Sacred Heart of thy divine Son.

LITANY OF ST. ALOYSIUS GONZAGA

V: Lord, have mercy on us.

R: *Christ, have mercy on us.*

Lord, have mercy on us. Christ, hear us.

Christ, graciously hear us.

God the Father of Heaven, *have mercy on us.*

God the Son, Redeemer of the world*

God, the Holy Ghost, the Sanctifier,*

Holy Trinity, One God*

Holy Mary, †*Pray for us.*

Holy Mother of God, †

Holy Virgin of virgins, †

Saint Aloysius Gonzaga†

Beloved child of Christ†

Delight of the Blessed Virgin†

Most chaste youth†

Angelic youth†

Most humble youth†

Model of young students†

Despiser of riches†

Enemy of vanities†

Scorner of honors†

Honor of princes†

Jewel of the nobility†

Flower of innocence†

Ornament of a religious state†

Mirror of mortification†

Mirror of perfect obedience†

Lover of evangelical poverty†

Most affectionately devout†

Most zealous observer of rules†

Desirous of the salvation of souls†

Perpetual adorer of the Holy Eucharist†

Particular client of Saint Ignatius†

Be merciful: *Spare us, O Lord.*

Be merciful: *Hear us, O Lord.*

From the concupiscence of the eyes: *O Lord, deliver us.*

From the concupiscence of the flesh: *O Lord, deliver us.*

From the pride of life: *O Lord, deliver us.*

Through the merits and intercessions of St. Aloysius: *O Lord, deliver us.*

Through his angelic purity: *O Lord, deliver us.*

Through his sanctity and glory: *O Lord, deliver us.*

Lamb of God, Who takes away the sins of the world, *have mercy on us, Lord.*

Lamb of God, Who takes away the sins of the world, *graciously hear us, Lord.*

Lamb of God, Who takes away the sins of the world, *have mercy on us, Lord.*

Christ, hear us. Christ, graciously hear us.

V: Pray for us, Saint Aloysius,

R: *That we may be made worthy of the promises of Christ.*

Let us pray. O God, Who, in distributing Thy heavenly gifts, didst in the angelic youth Aloysius, unite wonderful innocence of life with an equal spirit of penance: grant through his merits and prayers that we, who have not followed him in his innocence, may imitate him in his penance. Through our Lord Jesus Christ. Amen.

June 15th — *The Sacred Heart Of Jesus, Our Director*

Protectors for this day: St. Raphael, and the Holy Disciples of the Sacred Heart, St. Francis Borgia, and St. John of God

PRACTICE: For this one day at least, (and perhaps you wish for the month), go to the Heart of Jesus, as to your Spiritual Director, begging of him to let you know your faults and imperfections. Say the Litany of the Sacred Heart (pg. 39), to beg grace to do whatever Jesus may require of you. *Recite the Aspiration on pg. 72*

Prayer: Sacred Heart of Jesus, speak to my heart.

June 16th — *The Sacred Heart Of Jesus, Our Refuge*

Protectors for this day: St. Stanislaus and St. Aloysius

PRACTICE: In all temptations and trials, flee for refuge into the Sacred Heart of Jesus; and though by your past infidelities you find it closed against you, "Fear not," go to Mary, and she will surely give you entrance. Say in the spirit with humble confidence the "Our Father" and "Hail Mary." *Recite the Aspiration on pg. 72*

Prayer: Sacred Heart of Jesus, refuge of all the Miserable, protect me. Mary, refuge of sinners, pray for me, your child.

June 17th — *The Sacred Heart Of Jesus, Wounded On The Cross For Our Love*

Protectors for this day: The Angels of Sts. Aloysius and Stanislaus

PRACTICE: Honor by every means the wounded Hearts of Jesus and Mary. Make with fervor and compunction the Act of Reparation to these blessed Hearts (pg. 42). Resolve with Catharine of Sienna rather to die than ever again renew their sorrow by willful sin. *Recite the Aspiration on pg. 72*

Prayer: Precious blood flowing from the wounded Heart of Jesus, wash away my grievous sins, purify and invigorate me.

June 18th — *The Sacred Heart Of Jesus, Our Friend*

Protectors for this day: The Angels of the order of Sts. Dominic and Thomas Aquinas

PRACTICE: In a visit to the Sacred Heart in the Holy Sacrament, examine well your heart: its attachments, aversions, desires, fears, and joys. Beg of Jesus to give you a new heart, a heart pure and detached from self and creatures. Honor, love, and serve all creatures for Jesus, and in Jesus. *Recite the Aspiration on pg. 72*

Prayer: Sacred Heart of Jesus, true and only friend, receive me into thy friendship.

June 19th — *The Sacred Heart Of Jesus, The Angel Of The Great Council*

Protectors for this day: The Angel of our Diocese, and Sts. Charles and Liguori

PRACTICE: In your daily affairs and occupations, beg the light of the Angel of the Great Council. Sometimes for a moment kneel before an image of the Sacred Heart, and say, "Lord, that I may see." If you have the good custom of wearing a medal of the Sacred Heart, press it frequently to your heart and lips. *Recite the Aspiration on pg. 72*

Prayer: Sacred Heart of Jesus, Angel of the Great Council directs me.

June 20th — *The Sacred Heart Of Jesus, Our Solitude*

Protectors for this day: The Angels of our Churches, and Sts. Benedict and Scholastica

PRACTICE: Spend this day in the spirit of reparation and gratitude to the Sacred Heart of Jesus, solitary on our altars. Visit in this spirit, especially at the hour when you think it generally most solitary. Say the Act of Reparation to the Sacred Heart (pg. 42). *Recite the Aspiration on pg. 72*

Prayer: Sacred Heart of Jesus, silent and solitary, give me the spirit of the interior life, all hidden in thee.

June 21st — The Sacred Heart Of Jesus, Our Oratory And Altar

Protectors for this day: The Angels of St. Aloysius and St. Stanislaus Kostka

PRACTICE: Say the Litany of the Sacred Heart (pg. 39), and beg the Spirit in prayer: "You wish for an altar on which to offer your sacrifice? Lay them on the Sacred Heart of Jesus," and beg of Mary and Joseph to present them in your name. Try to have as many sacrifices as you can. There can be no sanctity without mortification. *Recite the Aspiration on pg. 72*

Prayer: Blessed Heart of Jesus, be my altar and my oratory. Teach me how to pray.

June 22nd — The Sacred Heart Of Jesus, Our Treasure

Protectors for this day: The holy angels of our Family, and
St. Ursula and Holy Companions

PRACTICE: Profit this day, at least, of the treasure in your hands, the Sacred Heart of Jesus. Enrich yourself, draw plentifully from this mine of grace, for yourself, and for all those who are near and dear to you; for poor sinners, for the souls in Purgatory, especially of the Holy Sacrifice. At the offertory of the Holy Mass consecrate yourself anew to the Heart of Jesus, through Mary and Joseph. *Recite the Act of Consecration on pg. 27 & the Aspiration on pg. 72*

Prayer: Sacred Heart of Jesus, my Treasure, enrich my soul with thy graces.

June 23rd — The Sacred Heart Of Jesus, Our Home & Dwelling

Protectors for this day: The Thrones, and St. John of the Cross

PRACTICE: Let the Heart of Jesus be your home and your dwelling. Try to prepare your heart for this great favor. Pray to the Holy Spirit and say the "Memorare" (pg. 82) to beg light to know what bad habits and passions chiefly impede your entrance into the Heart of Jesus. Be faithful to the hours of entering in spirit this sacred dwelling: nine in the morning and four in the evening. *Recite the Aspiration on pg. 72*

Prayer: Who shall dwell in thy heart, O Lord? Oh! let me be one.

The Memorare

Remember, O most gracious Virgin Mary, that never was it known that anyone who fled to thy protection, implored thy help, or sought your intercession was left unaided. Inspired by this confidence, I fly unto thee, O Virgin of virgins, my mother; to thee do I come, before thee I stand, sinful and sorrowful. O Mother of the Word Incarnate, despise not my petitions, but in thy mercy hear and answer me. Amen.

June 24th — The Sacred Heart Of Jesus, Zealous For Souls

Protectors for this day: The Holy Angels of all those employed in gaining souls to Jesus, and St. John the Baptist

PRACTICE: Offer all your interior and exterior sufferings for the conversion of sinners. Be generous this day in honoring and imitating the zeal of the Heart of Jesus. Do what you can for the instruction of the ignorant, and to prevent the commission of sin. "Too happy should I be," said St.Ignatius, "if by all my labors I prevented the commission of one sin." *Recite the Aspiration on pg. 72*

Prayer: Sacred Heart of Jesus, zealous for souls, have mercy on all poor sinners.

June 25th — The Sacred Heart Of Jesus, The Tender Lover Of Youth

Protectors for this day: The Archangels, and St. Philip Neri

PRACTICE: Honor, this day, and the 25th of every month, the sacred Heart of this Divine Infant Jesus. Think that he directly says to you, "Child, give me thy heart." Make an offering of your heart and affections, three times today, to your Infant Savior. *Recite the Aspiration on pg. 72*

Prayer: The Sacred Heart of the infant Jesus, I love thee.

June 26th — The Sacred Heart Of Jesus, That So Tenderly Loved The Poor And Sick

Protectors for this day: The Holy Angels of all devoted to the service of the poor and sick, and Sts. Vincent de Paul and Catharine of Genoa

PRACTICE: With all the fervor of your soul, be of the Sacred Heart of Jesus, through the maternal Heart of Mary, the true spirit of charity. Assist some poor person according to your means. *Recite the Act of Consecration on pg. 27 & the Aspiration on pg. 72*

Prayer: Sacred Heart of Jesus, comfort of the afflicted, give me true charity. Health of the sick, pray for us.

June 27th — The Sacred Heart Of Jesus, Our Physician

Protectors for this day: The Holy Angels especially devoted to the Sacred Heart of Jesus, and St. Matilda

PRACTICE: Receive the Sacred Heart of Jesus this day in the Holy Communion, at least spiritually, as the physician of your soul. Confidently beg your cure. Ask pardon for having so often trusted in creatures rather than in the Hearts of Jesus and Mary. *Recite the Act of Consecration on pg. 27 & the Aspiration on pg. 72*

Prayer: Sacred Heart of Jesus, "whom you love is sick." Heart of Mary, health of the sick, pray for me.

June 28th — The Sacred Heart Of Jesus, Our Peace

Protectors for this day: The Holy Angels of Peace, and St. Elizabeth of Hungary

PRACTICE: Say the "Gloria in Excelsis" (pg. 84) in union with the Angels of Peace, begging of the Heart of Jesus, through the Heart of Mary, that peace promised to all of goodwill. Examine, before a picture of the Sacred Heart, what has until now disturbed the peace of your soul. *Recite the Aspiration on pg. 72*

Prayer: Sacred Heart of Jesus, give me peace. Heart of Mary, pray for me.

Gloria in Excelsis

Glory be to God on high. And on earth peace to people of good will. We praise you. We bless you. We adore you. We glorify you. We give you thanks for your great glory. Lord God, heavenly King, God the Father Almighty. Lord Jesus Christ, Only-begotten Son, Lord God, Lamb of God, Son of the Father. You who takes away the sins of the world, have mercy on us. You who takes away the sins of the world, receive our prayer. You who sits at the right hand of the Father, have mercy on us. For you alone are holy. You alone are the Lord. You alone, O Jesus Christ, are most high. With the Holy Spirit, in the glory of God the Father. Amen.

June 29th — *The Sacred Heart Of Jesus, Our Joy*

Protectors for this day: The Archangels, and Sts. Peter and Paul

PRACTICE: Beg of the Sacred Heart of Jesus to enlighten you, that you may see what are the usual subjects of your joy. See if they are like those of true children of God; if not, let this be the time for reparation. Pray to the Holy Spirit. *Recite the Aspiration on pg. 72*

Prayer: Heart of Jesus, the joy of Angels, have mercy on me. Heart of Mary, Cause of our joy, pray for me.

June 30th — *The Sacred Heart Of Mary, The First Devoted To The Sacred Heart Of Jesus, And Our Way Into The Divine Heart*

Protectors for this day: The Angels who have especially protected us during this month, and St. Joseph

PRACTICE: Now you have come to the close of this month of benediction, this harvest of the spiritual year; what are your feelings, your resolutions, your remorse, your gratitude, and your love? Tell all to the Heart of Jesus, review your protestations of fidelity in the service of Jesus. Say the Litany of the Sacred Heart (pg. 39) in atonement for all the faults of this month. *Recite the Aspiration on pg. 72*

Prayer: Sacred Hearts of Jesus and Mary, I give you my heart and soul.

Oh Sacred Heart of Jesus, I adore you! Amen!

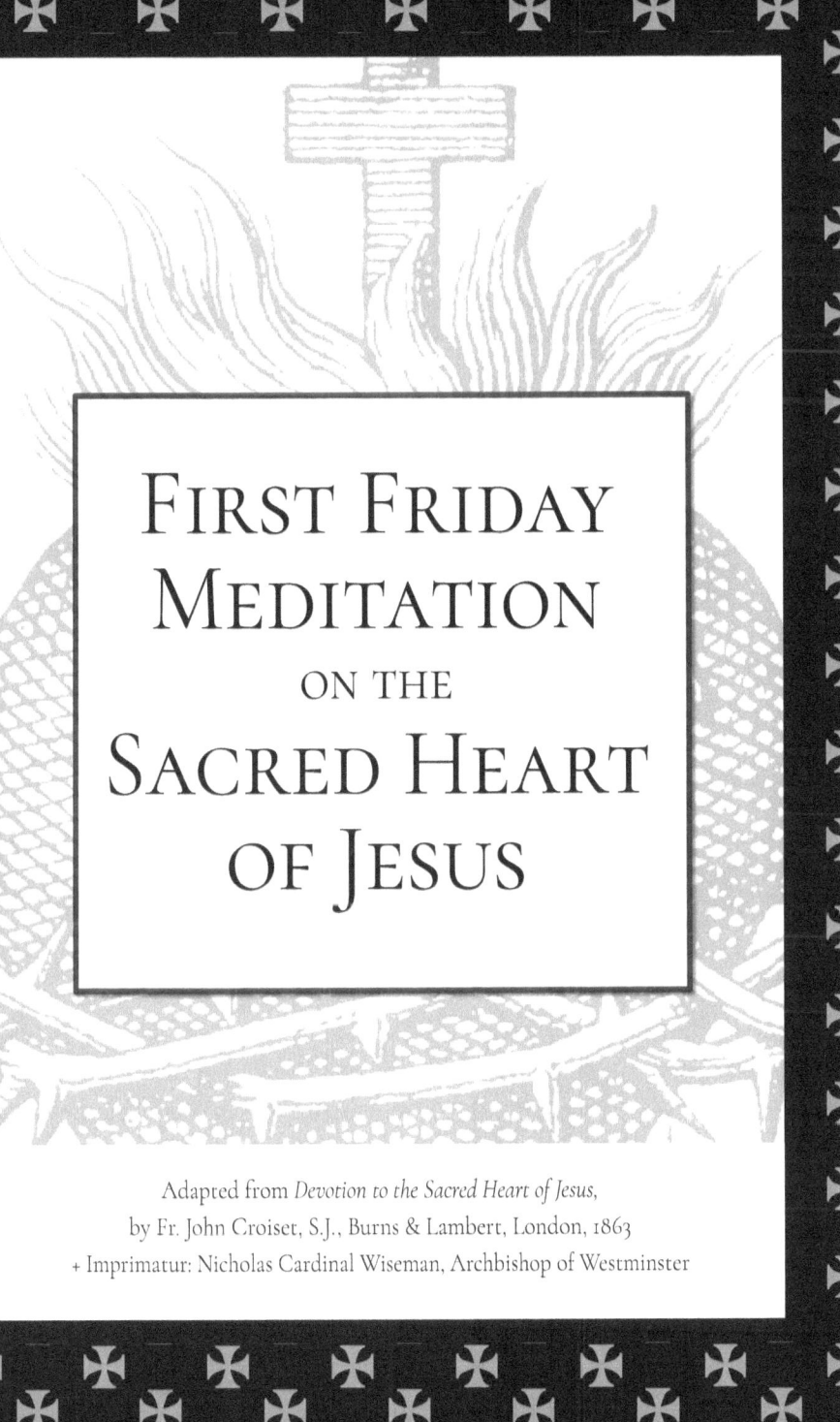

First Friday Meditation

on the

Sacred Heart of Jesus

Adapted from *Devotion to the Sacred Heart of Jesus,*
by Fr. John Croiset, S.J., Burns & Lambert, London, 1863
+ Imprimatur: Nicholas Cardinal Wiseman, Archbishop of Westminster

On the sentiments of the Heart of Jesus Christ at the sight of the ingratitude of men, and of the outrages, to which his excessive love for these very men has exposed him.

We may represent to ourselves the pitiable state to which the Son of God was reduced in the garden of Olives, when he allowed his imagination to bring before him, with the greatest liveliness possible, and with all the circumstances that added to his affliction, the greatness of his torments and the indignity of the insults he would have to endure, unto the end of ages, from three kinds of persons: from the Jews who would not acknowledge him; from heretics who, though they would acknowledge him, would not believe in his benefits; and from the faithful themselves, who, believing in him, would repay him only with ingratitude. At this sight he began to fear, as the Gospel tells us, to be sad and sorrowful, and at last he fell into a sort of agony, receiving no consolation from any one, not even from his faithful disciples, to whom he complained of it, when he said to them: "My soul is sorrowful unto death, and you forsake me, when you see me reduced to so miserable a state." Let us imagine that Jesus Christ is making this complaint to us.

First Point: The sentiments of the Heart of Jesus Christ at the sight of the torments he would have to endure, from the cruelty of the Jews.

Consider what were the sentiments of Jesus Christ, when he represented to himself distinctly on one hand the singular favors he had bestowed on this people, and on the other, the cruelties and the outrages that he would have to endure from this very nation after so many benefits. All the graces that had preceded his coming had been granted only in consideration of the merits of Jesus Christ. For that nation chiefly, the Son of God had become man. From it, in preference to any other, he had selected his relations and his friends, he had therein worked his miracles and preached his doctrine, yet for so many benefits he receives no return but harshness, persecution, and insults. Shelter is refused him when he is about to be born into the world. Almost as soon as he is born, he is obliged to seek refuge among strangers. How unworthily was he treated during his whole life? What did he not suffer at his death? He was taken like a thief, dragged like a culprit along those very streets through which, a few days before, he had been led in triumph as the Messiah. He was struck on the face as an insolent man in the house of Caiphas; he was spit upon as a blasphemer; he was treated with contempt and as a mock king; he was made for a whole night the butt of insolent soldiers, who assail him with insults; he was treated by Herod as an idiot and a fool; he was condemned to be scourged like a miserable slave—a criminal was preferred before him, as if he were the more wicked; lastly, he was condemned to the most ignominious of deaths, and nailed to a cross, on which he expires in the sight of a great number of persons, the greater part of whom had been witnesses of his miracles, and in whose favor he had worked them, without one person being found in all this number of people to take his part, or even to feel pity for him. They pass even from insensibility to contempt, and from contempt to horror and loathing. Are they are perhaps deceived? No, they are not deceived. They know very well how blameless his life has been, how holy and exemplary, miraculous, and filled with benefits and prodigies; and for this they persecute him.

All this presented itself clearly and distinctly to Jesus Christ. He knew well the dignity of his person, the greatness of his benefits, the disinterestedness of his love, the baseness, the rage, and the malice of those who treated him so cruelly.

A noble soul, when it is powerfully possessed by love, and hopes by suffering to make known its passion, is capable of offering itself spontaneously to torments; but the more generosity and tenderness it has, the more pain it feels in bearing injustice and ingratitude: especially when it sees itself sacrificed to the envy of its enemies, and betrayed by those from whom it had reason to expect help in its misfortunes, and when it sees that all that it suffers, is not capable of inspiring them with the smallest sentiment of compassion.

No one ever represented to himself events, with all their circumstances, more strongly or more distinctly than Jesus Christ. No one had ever a more generous heart, and consequently one more sensible to ingratitude. Oh God! with what a torrent of bitterness was this Sacred Heart then inundated, in representing to himself what he had done for this people, and what this people would do against him. Let us judge, who feel so deeply the least contempt, especially when it comes from those who are under some obligation to us, what must have been the feelings of Jesus Christ at such a spectacle.

The grief by which his Heart was oppressed, must have been very cruel, since it was the only torment of his Passion, of which Jesus Christ made any complaint. "My soul is sorrowful unto death," he said to his disciples, "and you forsake me, when you see me reduced to so pitiable a state!" Consider and see if there is a sorrow equal to mine. Oh ingratitude! Oh cruelty! And in so terrible an oppression, in such mortal sadness, no consolation. Ungrateful men! Insensible Christians! Is this your gratitude for your Savior, and for your God?

No, no, Lord; it shall never be true that you are so universally abandoned; it shall never be true that you cannot find any one to participate in your sorrow. I ask of Thee, oh Lord, that you would pour, from your Heart into mine, one drop of that torrent of bitterness with which you were inundated, at the sight of so much ingratitude and so many insults, that, if I am not happy enough, to be able to blot out my sins, by the shedding of all my blood, I may be at least afflicted enough to wash them away continually by my tears.

Second Point: The sentiment of the Heart of Jesus Christ at the sight of the outrages, which he should have to endure from the malice of heretics.

Consider that the second object of the fear, and of the terrible sadness in which the Heart of the Son of God was plunged was the number of the outrages and injuries that he would have to endure, from the malice of heretics to the end of ages, and which his imagination represented to him with all the circumstances that added to his affliction without diminishing them or concealing any of them from him. Nothing is more painful to a generous heart than ingratitude, especially when accompanied by great contempt. But the most enormous of all ingratitude is that by which man not only does not correspond with the benefits he has received, but even denies that he has ever received such benefits, in order to be at liberty to ill-use his benefactor, without being considered ungrateful. Jesus Christ knew distinctly at that time that there would be great numbers of Christians who would renew—in his sacred Body in the adorable Eucharist—all the outrages of which the malice of demons could be capable. That to be at liberty to exercise upon him all their fury and rage, they would carry their malice so far as to deny in the adorable Eucharist, the real presence of the Body of Jesus Christ.

Who would have believed that men could be capable of such excessive malice, and who can imagine anything more afflicting than to see that the most wonderful mark of the greatest love is made use of only to heap injuries on him, who has loved us so much? His imagination represented clearly to Jesus Christ, all that has happened in these latter ages. He saw his temples profaned, his altars demolished, his priests murdered, and his adorable Body thrown to the ground, trampled under foot, and made the object of the scoffs and insolence of the greatest sinners, the horror and the loathing of impious men.

What must have been the sentiments of this tender and generous Heart? Was it necessary, oh Lord, to work so great a miracle as to furnish men with a means of treating Thee so unworthily? Was it necessary, through an excess of love, to remain with them unto the end of ages, to be until the end of ages the object of their contempt and of their rage? Is not such a picture, enough to wither a heart with grief and sadness? O King of glory, are you he whom I see in so many places covered with insult and ignominy? Are you the God of Majesty before whom the Seraphim bow down with respect, whom I see so insolently treated by the wretched worms of the earth? Are you an object of horror and loathing to your creatures, to your slaves, to your own children, and all this because you have loved them too much?

Who could ever have imagined, that there would be in man an excess of malice, equivalent to the excess of your goodness, an excess of ingratitude corresponding so to speak with the excess of love with which you have loved us?

But, my beloved Savior, should not I be guilty of worse ingratitude if, in considering your sentiments at the sight of such cruel ingratitude, I were myself insensible to your grief?

Here is the place, oh Lord, where I see you, as your prophet has described you: the last of men, the man of sorrows (Isaiah 53:3). Heretics have treated you as the last and most contemptible of men, and have fulfilled the prophecy which said that you should be satiated with insults. But oh my God, will these heretics, these inhuman children, these impious men, never be satisfied with treating you so insolently, with offering you such outrages? And shall I never be touched by seeing you so ill-treated? This sad picture, this sight made you even sweat blood. I beg of you that it may move me to tears, and that if my heart cannot feel that grief which oppressed yours, the confusion I feel at being so insensible to your sufferings may supply in some degree for my insensibility.

Third Point: The sentiments of the Heart of Jesus Christ at the sight of the ingratitude of the greater number of the faithful.

Consider that it was no less an object of affliction and sadness for Jesus Christ to see the ingratitude of the greater number of the faithful themselves, who would show only coldness, indifference, and forgetfulness towards this most loving Savior. He saw the little esteem, not to say contempt, that would be felt for the greatest proof of the most ardent love. He saw that whatever he might do to be loved by the faithful, and to be continually with them by instituting the adorable Eucharist, neither this excess of love, nor his benefits, nor even his presence would have power to oblige them to love him, nor to prevent them from forgetting him. He represented to himself those churches wherein he dwells for the greater part of the time without adorers. He foresaw the want of respect and reverence with which persons would behave in his presence. He saw clearly how many would be found, who, losing entire hours in vain conversation, or useless visits, or spending the greater part of the day in idleness, would never find time, or rather would never be inclined to spend a quarter of an hour at the foot of his altars. Lastly, how many who would not be induced to visit him at all, and who would scarcely go once in eight days to adore him with coldness. He knew how many others would visit him without devotion, and how much irreverence and formality there would be in these visits; and lastly how few would visit him with eagerness. This loving Savior knew distinctly that the greater number would trouble themselves no more about him than if he were not upon earth or as if when on earth, he were not the same as in Heaven.

When he foresaw that Jews, Gentiles, and heretics would feel nothing for him but hardness and contempt, this bad treatment caused him extreme pain; but, after all, these are his declared enemies: and what do we expect from an enemy? But, what pained him most was that those who acknowledge his benefits, that the little flock which professes fidelity towards him, that his own children should be insensible to his benefits, and should not be touched at the sight of the grief caused him by these insults, nay should also despise him by their irreverences and sacrileges. "If Gentiles, Turks, and men who are professedly wicked, had vomited forth abuse against me, I would have borne it without complaining," might the loving Savior say. "But that Christians, Catholics, of whom I have been not only the Redeemer, but am still the daily food; that my own children should feel nothing for me but indifference, that they should even treat me with contempt!"

At this sight, at this thought, what were the sentiments of the Heart of Jesus Christ? That is, of the most tender and generous Heart that ever existed; of a Heart that loves the hearts of men passionately, and who meets in the hearts of these very men with nothing but coldness, hardness, and contempt. He says by the mouth of his prophet: "I have been made the sport and the laughing-stock of my enemies. At least amidst the insults that I have received, I should have met with a great number of servants and devoted friends, but it is quite the contrary. Scarcely did I disguise myself under the feeble forms of bread, to which the excess of my love has reduced me for the sake of the pleasure of being continually with men, than they removed further from me, they forsook me, they forgot me as one who had no place in their heart."

But did our loving Savior, in representing all this to himself, exaggerate the cause of his grief and sadness? Did this frightful picture deceive him, which placed before him so many insults and outrages, and so extraordinary an insensibility in the hearts of so many Christians? Is it then true that Jesus Christ has been treated like this? Is it true that his people have been insensible to this ill-treatment? Alas! It is enough for me to reflect on my own sentiments, and am not I a prodigy of insensibility, if in considering all this, I am still unmoved? Ah Lord! Can I think of all this, and at the same time reflect that it is a God who suffered this fearful sadness in which his Heart was plunged at the sight of so much insult and dishonor, that it is a God who willingly accepted and bore this opprobrium and this disgrace for me, and not die of grief and love? If a man or a slave, had suffered the hundredth part of what Jesus Christ has endured, and still bears daily on our altars, for the love of us, we could not refuse to love him, to be grateful to him, to give him at least marks of compassion, and to say sometimes: "That poor unhappy man really loved me, and he would not have borne so much if he had not loved me so dearly." Shall it be only the proofs of the love of Jesus Christ, still daily forgotten and despised in the adorable Eucharist, ill-treated for the love of us, to which we shall be insensible, and which we shall repay only by ingratitude and coldness? Can it be that the heart of man is capable of such an excess of hardness and insensibility? Alas! Lord, it is but too capable of it, and it will soon give proof of it, if that love which has obliged you to expose yourself to such indignities and outrages for it does not force you to soften its hardness, and warm its coldness, to make it feel its injuries to you, and render it capable of your love. For of what use would be all the miracles you have wrought, and all the torments you have endured, but to harden and make me more guilty, if I were not touched by them, if I did not feel grateful, and if I did not love you more in consequence? As I hope, oh Lord, that you will not refuse me your grace, I make at this moment a strong resolution to give you in the future undoubted proofs of my love, and of my just gratitude. I have been until now insensible to your benefits, insensible to your sufferings, indifferent towards you, though I know that you are continually with us. I have great reason, my loving Savior, to feel timidness in my promises and resolutions, having been previously so inconstant and unfaithful in your service; but it seems to me that your mercy now inspires me with greater courage that I may be in the future more constant and faithful in the promise I make you. That I may show by my respect in your presence, by my frequent visits, and by my close attention in attending upon you the sincere devotion I feel to your Sacred Heart. Further that the ardent desire I entertain of repairing as far as possible, during the rest of my days, all the contempt and the outrages you have endured in the adorable Eucharist by my respect and every kind of homage. May I also repair the forgetfulness and the extraordinary indifference that are shown towards your adorable person in the Blessed Sacrament.

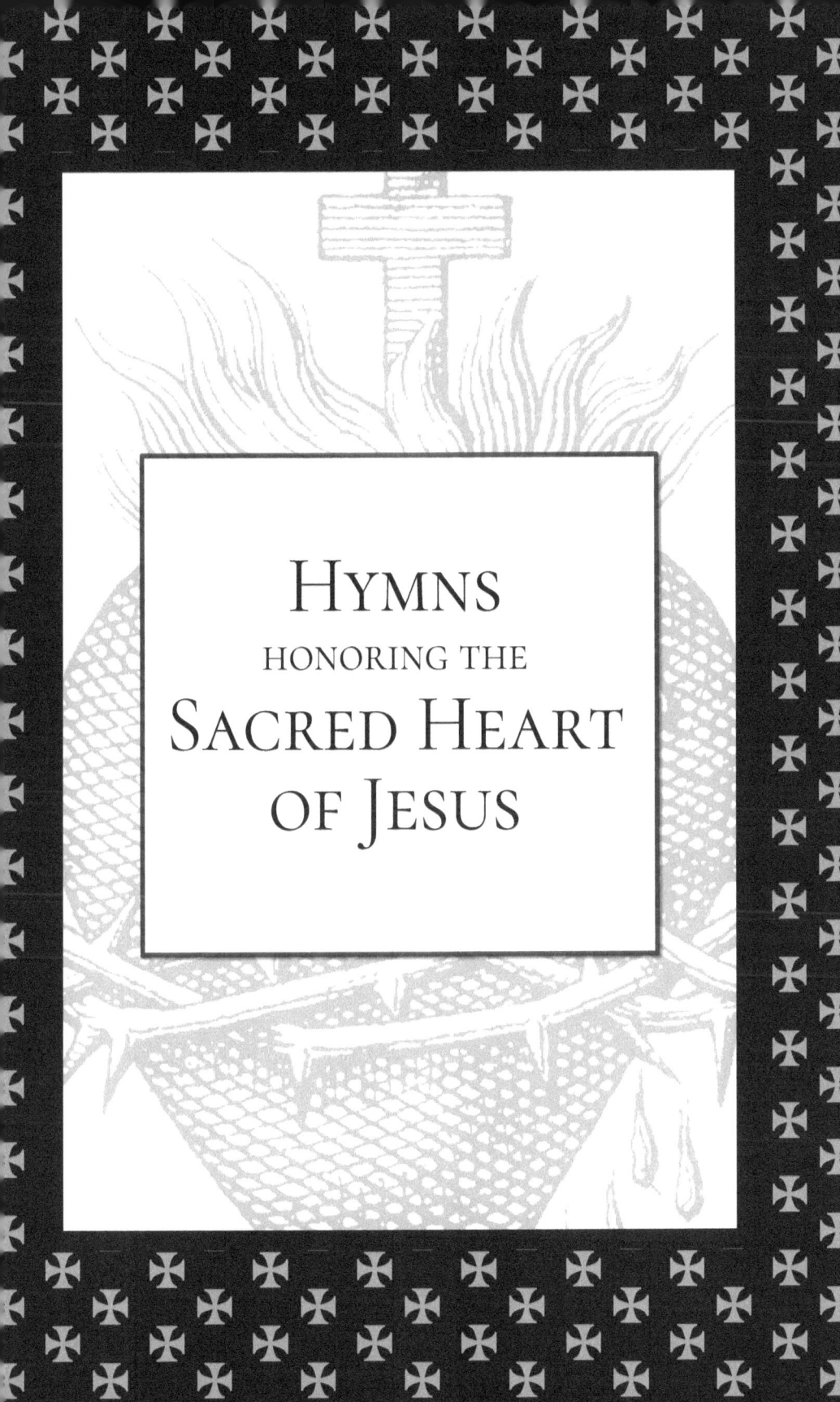

HYMNS
HONORING THE
SACRED HEART
OF JESUS

List of Hymns

O SACRED HEART, LET ALL THE EARTH

THE CATHOLIC HYMNAL BY REV. ALFRED YOUNG — 1888

1. O Sacred Heart, let all the earth Join with the heavens a-bove,
And eve-ry voice with sweet-est notes Pro-claim thy death-less love.
Come, Christians, come, and see how sin The Lord of love has slain;
Crave pardon of his Sa-cred Heart, And nev-er sin a-gain. A-men.

2 Sweet, patient, kind and loving Lord,
My sins have wounded Thee;
O take me to thy Sacred Heart,
Its Love will pardon me.
O Christians, see what grievous wounds
For love your Saviour bore;
Take refuge in His Sacred Heart,
And you will sin no more.

3 Friendless I stand beside thy cross,
In guilt and misery;
O take me to thy wounded Heart,
Its Love will comfort me.
Come, Christians, come and see what sin
Against your Lord could do;
Then look into his Heart, and see
What He hath done for you.

4 Homeless, amid this stormy world,
  Far have I strayed from Thee;
  Open to me thy Sacred Heart,
  Its Love will shelter me.
  Come, Christians, come and see how sin
  The Lord of love has slain;
  Crave pardon of his Sacred Heart,
  And never sin again.

5. Yes, take me, bind me, Lord of love,
  And hide me in thy breast;
  No other love can give such bliss,
  And only there is rest!
  O Christians! see what grievous wounds
  For love your Saviour bore;
  Come, hide within his Sacred Heart,
  And we will sin no more.   Amen.

Lo! How the Cruel Power

THE CATHOLIC HYMNAL BY REV. ALFRED YOUNG — 1888

1. Lo! how the cru-el power Of our proud sins hath rent The Heart of our all-gra-cious God, That Heart so in-no-cent! A-men.

2 O wounded Heart! whence sprang
  The Church, the Saviour's Bride;
  Thou Door of our salvation's Ark
  Set in its mystic side!

3 Thou holy Fount, whence flows
  The sacred seven-fold flood,
  Where we our robes defiled may cleanse
  In the Lamb's saving Blood.

4 By sorrowful relapse
  Thee will we rend no more;
  But like thy flames, those types of love,
  Strive heavenward to soar.

5 Father and Son supreme,
  And Spirit, hear our cry!
  Whose is the kingdom, praise and power,
  Through all eternity.   Amen.

JESU, CREATOR OF THE WORLD

THE CATHOLIC HYMNAL BY REV. ALFRED YOUNG — 1888

1. Je - su, Cre - a - tor of the world, Of all man - kind Redeem - er blest! True God of God, in whom we see The
Fa - ther's im - age clear ex - pressed. A - - men.

2 Thee, Saviour, Love alone constrained
   To make our mortal flesh thine own;
   And as a second Adam come,
   For the first Adam to atone.

3 That self-same Love which made the
   sky,   [earth,
   Which made the sea, and stars, and
   Took pity on our misery,
   And broke the bondage of our birth.

4 O Jesu! in thy Heart divine
   May that same love for ever glow;
   For ever mercy to mankind
   From that exhaustless Fountain flow.

5 For this thy Sacred Heart was pierced,
   And both with Blood and Water
   ran;
   To cleanse us from the stains of guilt,
   And be the strength and hope of man.

6 To God the Father, and the Son,
   All praise and power and glory be,
   With Thee, O Holy Comforter,
   Henceforth through all eternity. Amen.

O Jesus, Open Wide Thy Heart

The Catholic Hymnal by Rev. Alfred Young — 1888

1. O Jesus, open wide thy heart, And let me rest therein; For weary is my stricken soul Of sorrow and of sin. O Jesu, Jesu! Victim blest, What else but Love Divine Could Thee constrain to open thus That Sacred Heart of thine? Amen.

2 O Veil of awful mystery!
  O Temple all sublime!
Thou Sanctuary, holier far
  Than that of olden time.
O Fount of endless Life and Joy!
  O Spring of waters clear!
O Flame celestial, cleansing all
  Who unto Thee draw near.

3 Beneath this emblem of pure love,
  'Twas Love Himself that died,
And offered up Himself for us,
  A Victim crucified.

Blest Heart of Christ, in thy dear wound
  The hidden depth we see
Of what we else could never know—
  His boundless charity.

4 Oh, who of his redeemed will Him
  Their mutual love refuse?
Who would not rather in that Heart
  Their home eternal choose?
Yes, take me to that Place of Rest,
  And seal the entrance o'er,
That from that home my wayward heart
  May never wander more. Amen.

O CHRIST, THE WORLD'S CREATOR BRIGHT

St. Basil's Hymnal — 1918

FR. F. C. HUSENBETH

T. W. STANIFORTH

Moderato (♩ = 88)

1. O Christ, the world's Cre - a - tor bright, Who
2. Thy love com-pelled Thee to as - sume A

didst man-kind from sin re - deem, The Fa - ther's ev - er -
mor - tal Bo - dy man to save; Re - ver - sing ol - den

glo - rious Light, True God of God, in bliss su - preme.
Ad - am's doom, The New - er Ad - am ran - som gave.

3.
That love which once created all,
The earth, the stars, the wondrous sea,
Took pity on our parents' fall,
Broke all our bonds and set us free.

4.
O Saviour, let Thy potent love
Flow ever from Thy bounteous heart;
To nations that pure fount above
The grace of pardon will impart.

5.
To God the Father, to the Son
And to the Holy Ghost the same
Be glory, power, while ages run,
And endless rule in endless fame.

O Christ Behind Thy Temple's Veil

St. Basil's Hymnal — 1918

BREVIARY LATIN

S. WEBBE

Moderato (♩ = 104)

1. O Christ, be-hind Thy Tem-ple's veil, En-closed in ark of gold, On stones en-gra-ven, lay the law Thy fin-ger wrote of old.——

2. In-car-nate Word in Tem-ple new, Thy Life-Blood's throb-bing Shrine On flesh-y ta-bles gra-ven held The law of love di-vine.——

3.

And when that Heart in death was still'd,
Each temple's veil was riven,
And lo, within Thy loves red shrine
To us to look was given.

4.

There make us gaze, and see the love
Which drew Thee, for our sake,
O great High-Priest, Thyself to God
A Sacrifice to make.

5.

Thou, Saviour, cause that every soul,
Which Thou hast loved so well,
May will within Thine opened heart
In life and death to dwell.

6.

O grant it, Father, only Son
And Spirit God of grace,
To Whom all worship shall be done
In every time and place.

ONLY THEE, MY JESUS

St. Basil's Hymnal — 1918

M. S. PINE

Adapted from HAYDN

Moderato (♩ = 80)

1. On - ly Thee, my Je-sus, On-ly Thee I crave; Thou didst loose my
2. How can I re-pay Thee? Grac-es ev - ery hour Thrill my soul with

fet-ters, All my sins for-gave. Here to Thine own tem-ple Thou hast led my
won-der, Tell Thy love and power. On-ly Thee my Je - sus! Thine are all my

feet; To Thy Heart hast bound me By love's fet-ters sweet. On-ly Thee my Je-sus
days, Vowed to Thee for - ev - er, Thine is all my praise.

CHORUS

Thou art all to me; Soul and heart are sing-ing Je-sus on-ly Thee!

3.
Bowed in Thy sweet presence,
Fleet the hours divine;
While Thy Heart is whispering
"Let thy heart be Mine."
Then to labor hasting
I am still with Thee,
And Thy voice still lingers;
"Teach and toil for Me?"
Cho. Only Thee, *etc.*

4.
O! the bliss of knowing
Jesus, I am Thine;
Naught from Thee can sever,
Naught but sin of mine.
O'er the earth, o'er angels
Do I take my flight;
Only Thee, my Jesus!
Thou art life and light.
Cho. Only Thee, *etc.*

O Sacred heart, That On The Cross

St. Basil's Hymnal — 1918

EV. J. TALBOT SMITH

Largo (♩ = 60)

1. O Sa-cred Heart, that on the Cross, Gave up Thy lat-est breath for me; This
2. From Beth-le-hem to Calv'ry's hour, Thy beat-ings were for me a-lone; Yet

hour of song and sac - ri-fice, With will - ing mind I give to Thee.
have I scorned its gen-tle power, For all Thy ma - ny fav-ours shown.

CHORUS Piu animato

O Sac-red Heart, sweet Sac-red Heart, Shrine of our faith, tem-ple of love,

O Sac-red Heart, sweet Sac-red Heart, Bring us to Thee in heav'n a-bove.

3.
With deep resolve I turn to Thee,
And pardon ask for every sin,
My heart henceforth shall beat with Thine,
Nor let the slightest evil in.

4.
O give me grace to do Thy will,
And keep my soul from every stain;
That when my last sad hour has come,
I may not look to Thee in vain.

I Dwell A Captive In This Heart

St. Basil's Hymnal — 1918

Moderato (♩ = 84)

L. BERG

1. I dwell a cap-tive in this heart In-flamed with love di - vine; 'Tis
2. Here like the dove with-in the ark, Se-cure-ly I re-pose; Sinc

here I live a - lone in peace, And con-stant joy is mine.__
now the Lord is my de-fence, I fear no earth-ly foes.__

DUET ad lib.

It is the heart of God's own Son In His hu-man-i - ty, __ Who
What tho' I suf - fer, still in love I ev - er true will be; __ My

all en-am-our'd of my soul, Here burns with love of me.__ I
love of God shall deep-er grow When cross - es fall on me.__ Here

3.

From every bond of earth, O Lord,
Thy grace hath set me free;
My soul delivered from the snare
Enjoys true liberty.
Nought more can I desire than this,
To see Thy face in heav'n;
And this I hope, since He on earth
His heart in pledge hath giv'n.

106

MY DEAREST SAVIOR I WOULD FAIN

St. Basil's Hymnal — 1918

r. Dr. H. T. HENRY

Anon

Andante (♩ = 80)

1. My dear - est Sav - iour I would fain With
2. In vain the de - mon lays his snares, In

in Thy Sa - cred Heart re - main: O let me safe a -
vain the bribe of world-ly wares: He can-not tempt a

bide For - ev - er in Thy Wound - ed Side.
pride For - got - ten in Thy Wound - ed Side.

From Treasury of Catholic Song.

3.

And though the flesh wage war my soul
In guilty pleasures to control,
For me is opened wide
The portal of Thy Wounded Side.

4.

When fading sight and fluttering breath
Proclaim the near approach of death,
O Saviour, let me hide
And die within Thy Wounded Side.

PITY, MY GOD, 'TIS FOR OUR LOVED LAND

ST. BASIL'S HYMNAL — 1918

Traditional

Largo (♩ = 44)

1. Pi - ty my God; 'tis for our lov - ed land,
2. Our err - ing souls, so long es - tranged from truth,

And for Thy Church we hum-bly bow in prayer: Thy Vi-car's cap - tive,
Look up for sol - ace to Thy sa-cred Throne; Light up their faith, that,

break his prison band, Thy Church's loss - es in Thy might re-pair.
like the eagle's youth, It be renewed, and shine as once it shone.

CHORUS

God of migh-ty power Take Thy Vicar's part: Oh, save him in this hour For

Je-sus' Sacred Heart, Oh save him in this hour For Je-sus' Sacred Heart.

3.

Pity, my God; on those misguided men
Who outrage Thee, but know not what they do;
In mercy wait, and draw them back again,
Their faith and love in sorrow to renew.

108

Peace, Be Still! Our God is Dwelling

St. Basil's Hymnal — 1918

Andante (♩ = 76)

1. Peace be still! our God is dwell-ing Si-lent on His al-tar throne; Let us
2. Thou hast called the hea-vy-la - den, Called the poor, the frail to Thee, See us

kneel, our bo-soms swell - ing, With a joy but sel-dom known. Heart of
then, O Son of Maid - en! None could poor-er, frail-er be, Thou dost

Je - sus! come we hith - er, With our bur-dens meek - ly in, From a
know the woes and weak-ness Of a na - ture prone to ill, Heart of

world where spir-its with - er, From a world whose breath is sin.
mer - cy! Heart of meek-ness! Be our shield, our suc - cour still!

CHORUS

Heart of Je - sus! strength su-per-nal! Send us pow-er from a - bove; Heart of

Je - sus! light e - ter - nal! Fill our souls with light and love!

109

Sacred Heart in Accents Burning

St. Basil's Hymnal — 1918

Andante (♩ = 72)

1. Sa - cred Heart, in ac - cents burn-ing, Pour we forth our love of
2. Heart of boun - ty, Thou art bring-ing All Thy thirst-ing chil-dren

Thee; Hear our hopes and hear our yearn - ings Meet and
here, Where the liv - ing wat - ers spring-ing, Tell of

min - gle ten - der - ly. Heart of mer - cy, ev - er
hope and com - fort near! O Thou Source of ev - 'ry

ea - ger All our woes and wounds to heal; Heart most
bless - ing! Sweet-est, strong - est, holi - est, best! Be our

pa - tient, Heart most pure, To our souls Thy depths re - veal.__
treas - ure here on earth, And in Heav'n be Thou our rest!__

CHORUS

Sa-cred Heart of our Re - deem - er! Pierced with love on Cal-va -

- ry; Heart of Je - sus ev - er lov - ing, Make us

burn with love of Thee. Praise to Thee! Sa - cred Heart.

Upon the Altar, Night and Day

St. Basil's Hymnal — 1918

Andantino (♩. = 56)

1. Up - on the al - tar, night and day, The Heart of Je - sus lies, — And night and day through out the world, Do men Its claims des - pise; — For by their cold un - grate-ful lives, They pierce it through and through, And

2. Be - neath a crown of cru - el thorns, Thy Heart is all on fire; — And bright - ly shines from out Its flames, The cross of Thy de - sire. — If pure and true must be the soul That fain would hide in Thee, Oh!

by the scour-ges of their crimes, Its ag - o-nies re - new. __
let Thy roy - al love sup - ply, For all our mi - se - ry! __

O draw us close to Thee, sweet Lord! And
Then draw us clo - ser still 'to Thee, O

burn - ing zeal im - part, __ To now re - pair, by
Sa - cred Heart Di - vine! __ In joy and grief, in

praise and pray'r, The wrongs of Thy Dear Heart!
life and death, Our hearts are ev - er Thine.

3.

We offer Thee our humble gifts,
   For poor they are and small,
Our hearts, our souls, our little lives,
   Dear Heart! we give Thee all;

And joyous victims we shall be,
   Consumed before Thy Throne,
If dead to sin, if dead to self,
   We live to Thee alone!

O Jesus, Lord, Most Mighty King

St. Basil's Hymnal — 1918

Tr. J. D. AYLWARD, O. P.

ST. BERNARD

S. WEBBE Jr.

Cantabile (♩ = 92)

1. O Je - sus, Lord, most migh - ty King And Con - que-
2. When Thou art in my heart, the world With all its

ror di - vine, ___ O Sweet - ness in - fi -
pomp de - cays, ___ The truth shines bright, and

nite, for Whom Our souls un - ceas - ing pine. ___
love lights up Its rea - dy kin - dled blaze. ___

3.
O Jesus, sweetness of the heart,
Thou Living Spring of Light,
So far exceeding all desire,
All joys of sense or sight.

4.
O dearest Jesus, let me feel
The fulness of Thy love,
And cleanse mine eyes to see Thy face
In Thy bright courts above.

5.
O Jesus, brighter than the sun,
O Balm with healing blest,
Of all things sweet, of all things fair,
Thou sweetest, fairest, best.

114

O Sacred Heart! O Love Divine!

St. Basil's Hymnal — 1918

Andante (♩.= 58)

1. O Sa-cred Heart! O Love Di-vine! Do keep us near to Thee; And
2. O Tem ple pure! O House of gold! Our heav-en here be - low! What

make our love so like to Thine That we may ho - ly be.
sweet de-lights, what wealth un-told, From Thee do ev - er flow.

CHORUS

Heart of Je - sus hear! O Heart of Love Di - vine!

Lis - ten to our prayer; Make us al - ways Thine.

3.
O wounded Heart, O Font of tears!
O Throne of grief and pain!
Whereon for the eternal years,
Thy love for man does reign.

4.
Ungrateful hearts, forgetful hearts,
The hearts of men have been,
To wound Thy side with cruel darts
Which they have made by sin.

A Message From the Sacred Heart

St. Basil's Hymnal — 1918

Rev. M. Russell S.J.

Moderato (♩ = 104)

1. A message from the Sacred Heart! What may this message be? "My
2. A message to the Sacred Heart! Oh bear it back with speed; Come

child my, child! give Me thy heart; My heart has bled for thee," This
Jesus, reign within my heart, Thy heart is all I need." This

is the message Jesus sends To my poor heart to-day, And
prayer I'll pray while here I pine, From Heaven and Thee a-part, Nor

from His Throne in heaven He bends To hear what I shall say.
cease, dear Lord, till I am Thine For-ev-er, heart to heart.

FROM YOUR RANKS

ST. BASIL'S HYMNAL — 1918

Andante Moderato (♩. = 63)

ZARDIUNI

1. Form your ranks O all ye Leaguers of the Heart di-vine, Fight your
2. Christian men and Christian maidens and ye faithful all, Come and

bat-tles with the migh-ty arms of pray'r, And your conq'ring hosts shall
wor-ship the sweet Heart of Christ our King; See how Je-sus has re-

gath-er round the ho-ly shrine, Crown'd as victors by the King Whose love we share.
paired the guilt of A-dam's fall, And the glo-ry of such love we'll grateful sing.

CHORUS

Heart of Je-sus___ with love for us burn-ing,___ Make us

love Thee more and more with ev'-ry day.___ Heart of day.

3
Lo! Thy Heart, O dear Redeemer, is a furnace fierce,
Ever burning with the fire of love divine!
Grant that ever thru our hearts this heav'nly fire may pierce,
And transform them into loving hearts like Thine.

4
How ungrateful we have been in all the years gone by,
For Thy mercies and Thy graces freely given!
Heart of Jesus Which so often we have caused to sigh,
Add repentance as our final gage to Heaven.

I RISE FROM DREAMS OF TIME

ST. BASIL'S HYMNAL — 1918

1. I rise from dreams of time, And an an - gel guides my feet ___ To the Sa - cred Al - tar Throne Where Je - sus' Heart doth beat, To the Sa - cred Al - tar Throne Where Je - sus Heart doth beat. ___

2. The love lamp soft - ly burns And a won - drous si - lence reigns ___ On - ly with a low still voice The Ho - ly One com - plains, On - ly with a low still voice The Ho - ly One com - plains. ___

3
Ever pleading day and night,
Thou can'st not from us part,
O veil'd and wondrous Son,
    O Love of the Sacred Heart,
O veil'd and wondrous Son,
    O Love of the Sacred Heart.

118

O Jesus Dear, Thy Sacred Heart

St. Basil's Hymnal — 1918

Moderato (♩ = 92)

1 O Je -sus Dear, Thy Sa-cred Heart Is fraught with purest Love; Much
2 Thy Sa-cred Heart for-ev - er glows For pen-i-tents sin - cere; It

joy to me Thou dost im - part, And com - fort from a - bove.
proves thy ten-der-ness that flows To hear and grant my pray'r.

O Sa-cred Heart, ce-les-tial feast Of all the bless'd a - bove, I
Tis true my sins for vengence cry, And draw me to des - pair; But

hope in bliss Thy sweets to taste, And glow with heav'nly love.
to Thy Sa-cred Heart I'll fly, To find my re - fuge there.

3

Thy Sacred Heart was pierced for me,
 And bled at every pore!
From past offences set me free,
 Oh! them I shall deplore.
My tears shall never cease to flow
 Because from Thee I've strayed,
Who with such weight of pain and woe
 My ransom freely paid.

4

O! let me kiss Thy sacred feet,
 Thy bleeding hands and side;
To suffer pain for Thee is meet,
 Who freely for me died.
O Sacred Heart, celestial feast,
 Of all the bless'd above,
I hope in bliss Thy sweets to taste
 And glow with heav'nly love

How Shall I Ever Know the Love

St. Basil's Hymnal — 1918

Maestoso, non lento (♩ = 80)

1 How shall I ev - er now the love Thou hast, O God, for me?
2 As God, Thou loved'st me be - fore The world or time be-gan:

Nor men be-low, nor saints a - bove, That love can tell or see.
And now, as if to love me more, Thou lov - est me as man.

Nor An-gels know, nor heav-en's Queen, The lov - ing God Thou art;
It seems, dear Lord, Thou would'st forsake Thy glo - ry to im - part

Thy love is on - ly felt and seen By Je - su's Sa-cred Heart.
Thy life to me, when Thou didst take A liv - ing hu-man Heart.

CHORUS

O Heart of Je- sus! I im -plore That I may love Thee more and more.

3
The earth beneath, the heaven above,
Thy mercy would entwine,
To thus unite in links of love
The human and divine.
And so that in our griefs and joys
Thou mightest have a part,
And feel with us and sympathize,
Thou hast a human Heart

4
O Sacred Heart in Thee enshrined
Is all that angels prize;
Within Thy holy depths I find
My solace and my joys.
For Thee and for Thy love I yearn,
Teach me the heavenly art,
To be like Thee - Thy lessons learn,
O meek and humble Heart.

To Jesus' Heart All Burning

St. Basil's Hymnal — 1918

Rev. A. J. CHRISTIE S. J.   Traditional Air

Cantabile (♩ = 88)

1. To Je-sus' Heart all burn-ing With fer-vent love for men My
2. O Heart for me on fire, With love no man can speak, My

heart with fond-est yearn-ing shall raise the joy-ful strain.
yet un-told de - sire, God gives me for Thy sake.

REFRAIN

While a - ges course a - long, Blest be with loud-est song The

Sa - cred Heart of Je - sus By ev' - ry heart and tongue, The

Sa - cred Heart of Je - sus By ev' - ry heart and tongue.

3.
Too true I have forsaken
Thy flock by wilful sin,
Yet now let me be taken
Back to Thy fold again.

4.
As Thou art meek and lowly,
And ever pure at Heart,
So may my heart be wholly
Of Thine the counterpart.

O Sacred Heart! Our Home Lies Deep In Thee

St. Basil's Hymnal — 1918

REV F STANFIELD

STEVENSON

Andante Religioso (♩ = 88)

1. O Sa - cred Heart! Our home lies deep in Thee,
2. O Sa - cred Heart! Thou fount of con - trite tears,

On earth Thou art an ex - ile's rest,
Where - e'er those liv - ing wa - ters flow,

In heav'n the Glo - ry of the blest,
New life to sin - ners they be - stow,

dim. e rit.

O Sa - cred Heart! O Sa - cred Heart!
O Sa - cred Heart! O Sa - cred Heart!

3.
O Sacred Heart!
Bless our dear native land,
Her noble sons courageous stand
With faith's bright banner still in hand,
O Sacred Heart!

4.
O Sacred Heart!
Our trust is all in Thee;
For though earth's night be dark and drear,
Thou breathest rest where Thou art near,
O Sacred Heart!

5.
O Sacred Heart!
Lead exiled children home,
Where we may ever rest near Thee,
In peace and joy eternally;
O Sacred Heart!

O TAKE ME TO THY SACRED HEART

St. Basil's Hymnal — 1918

Sister of Notre Dame

1. Oh, take me to Thy Sa - cred Heart And seal the en - trance
2. Oh, Je - sus' Heart, meek, pa - tient, kind, My soul to Thee doth

o'er That from that home this wea - ry heart May nev-er wander more.
turn, Thou would'st not crush the bruis-ed reed, The sorrowing spir-it spurn.

CHORUS

Yes! Je - sus take me to Thyself, I'm wea - ry wait-ing here I

long to lean up - on Thy breast, To see, to feel Thee near.

3.
Oh, Jesus, open wide Thy Heart
  And let me rest therein
For weary is my stricken soul
  Of sorrow and of sin.

4.
I've sought for rest and found it not
  In things of earthly mould;
I pine to love and be beloved
  By that Heart that grows not cold.

5.
Oh, Mary, by the priceless love
  Which Jesus' Heart bore thee,
Pray that my home in life and death
  That loving Heart may be.

From Notre Dame Hymnal by per permission.

HEART OF JESUS, WE ARE GRATEFUL

ST. BASIL'S HYMNAL — 1918

Andante (♩. = 63)

1. Heart of Je - sus, we are grate - ful For Thy
2. Heart of Je - sus, Thou hast taught us How to

an - swer to our pray'r; We have sought Thee, ev - er
seek and how to find, And that les - son now has

hope - ful That Thy bless-ings we might share; Thou hast
brought us To Thy Heart so sweet and kind. What we

heard us in - ter - ced - ing, With Thy love which is un -
ask, with faith be - liev - ing, Thou hast pledged Thy word to

told, And in an - swer to our plead - ing All Thy
give, And Thy word is not de - ceiv - ing, But the

treas - ures dost un - fold. Heart of Je - sus, we will
truth by which we live. Heart of Je - sus, we will

thank Thee, We will love Thee more and more; Heart of
thank Thee, We will love Thee more and more; Heart of

Je - sus, we will praise Thee, and we'll thank Thee o'er and o'er.
Je - sus, we will praise Thee, and we'll thank Thee oer and oer.

3.
Heart of Jesus, whilst we waited
    For the favors now obtained,
Not a moment had we doubted
    That by prayer they'd be gained.
Thou hadst told us that our treasures
    Would be found in Thy dear Heart,
And we knew that without measure
    Thou dost all Thy gifts impart.

125

THE PERPETUAL LAMP

In many churches and chapels, by means of small contributions,
a lamp is kept burning day and night before the picture of the
Sacred Heart. The object and beautiful significance of this
custom is the subject of the following hymn.

This Lamp, though plain and poor It be, Yet burn day and night,

O Sacred Heart! to honor Thee, and sheds its mellow light.

And my poor heart, though far away, With ceaseless yearning turns,

To Thy dear shrine, with gentle ray, where this lamp ever burns.

O Lord! Inspirit prostrate here, I offer Thee its rays,

As adoration's constant prayer, Thanksgiving, love and praise.

And while through day with painful tramp; I plod my weary way,

Before Thy heart this little Lamp, for me shall homage pay.

When after toil repose I take, And night brings gentle sleep,

A loving vigil for my sake It evermore shall keep.

O, heart of Jesus! Meek and mild, Accept this gift, though poor,

And grant the grace to me, Thy child. To love Thee more and more.

To you who live in grief and pain, Oppressed by guilt's dismay,

May heavenly peace return again. To chase your griefs away.

Jesus on high, to sinner's kind, A victim doth appear;

O hasten his fond heart to find, And rest securely there.

Yes, 'tis his voice that sounds so sweet; Why, sinners, fly from Me?

Come, seek forgiveness at My feet, your sins shall pardon be.

What heart did ever friendship prove Like His, so good and great,

Behold how his expiring love his Father doth entreat.

For you and me, nay, e'en for those Who bid his veins to bleed:

"Father, forgive my cruel foes." O, this was love indeed.

Jesus, that Heart, which with delight Fills the angelic train,

Doth sweetly thus our souls invite Thy mercy to obtain.

O, dry our tears, our bruises heal. To us Thy blood applies:

A new-formed heart in us reveals, Who for Thy bounty cry.

Sacred heart of Jesus, dying on the Cross...
...*save me,*

Heart of my redeemer...
...*answer for me,*

Sacred Heart, retreat of afflicted souls...
...*comfort me,*

SAINTS

St. Anne	St. John Paul II	St. Michael the Archangel
St. Anthony of Padua	St. John the Baptist	St. Patrick
St. Benedict of Nursia	St. John the Evangelist	St. Paul
St. Catherine of Sienna	St. Joseph	St. Peter
St. Dominic	St. Luke the Evangelist	St, Thérèse of Lisieux
St. Frances Cabrini	St. Margaret of Castello	St. Thomas Aquinas
St. Francis of Assisi	St. Mark the Evangelist	St. Thomas the Apostle
St. Ignatius of Loyola	St. Matthew the Evangelist	... *And more coming soon*
St. Joan of Arc	St. Maximillian Kolbe	

BLESSED VIRGIN MARY

The Catholic Church celebrates five feasts in honor of the Blessed Virgin Mary. These Prayer Journals are a great resource to help deepen your connection to the Mother of God by celebrating these five feasts throughout the year. Available for the individual feasts, or as one volume—The Five Feast of Mary—that contains all five.

The Five Feasts of Mary	The Annunciation
The Immaculate Conception	The Seven Sorrows of Mary
The Nativity of Mary	The Assumption

www.ingramcontent.com/pod-product-compliance
Lightning Source LLC
Chambersburg PA
CBHW030302130626
46549CB00002B/658